P9-DHQ-725

Rural Ontario

RURAL ONTARIO

Verschoyle Benson Blake / Ralph Greenhill

University of Toronto Press

Printed in the United States of America
SBN 8020 1539 5

Contents

Introduction

The photographs collected in this book are intended to record an aspect of the older-settled, rural parts of Ontario, an aspect now being rapidly eroded by changing conditions. The collection is not intended to be a complete record, either of the rural landscape of Ontario or of its older buildings. Rather it is a sampling of what has pleased us in travelling over country roads, because a view or building seemed attractive in itself, was typical of some phase of rural life, or presented some feature of unusual interest.

It was, of course, necessary to impose some limitations of time and place, or the number of photographs would have exceeded all bounds. It was decided to interpret the word 'rural' somewhat strictly and avoid towns and larger villages. It soon became evident that, as far as buildings were concerned, subjects were likely to belong to the nineteenth century. To try to include representative examples later than 1900 would mean excluding more desirable examples of greater age. This was one of the reasons why we restricted our range to the older-settled parts of Ontario, neglecting the rocky and forested wildness of the Laurentian Shield. It was the charm of these countrysides that had particularly attracted us in the first place, and we felt that for several generations they had been little appreciated while the northern wildernesses had been extravagantly praised. Since we could not hope to make an adequate record of the whole province, we preferred to concentrate on those aspects which especially appealed to us and which had less often been recorded.

These restrictions were not intended to be inflexible rules, but they have on the whole been fairly strictly observed. Occasionally they constituted a certain handicap in finding subjects – for example when looking for the earlier types of building. Naturally most of the better buildings of the earlier period were either in villages or in places where villages and towns later grew up. Some of the best surviving examples of the frame house of this early period are found in places now too large for our definition of 'rural'.

This will explain some omissions in the collection. Others are due to a certain tendency, partly unconscious and not consistently followed, to avoid examples already well known and often illustrated. Other subjects of all sorts were encountered under conditions that made it impossible or difficult to obtain a satisfactory photograph; these could only be noted in the hope of a return at a different season or time of day. Such a return trip did not always prove possible, either for lack of time or because the collection threatened to exceed the required numbers. It is possible that a second, or even a third, collection could be made from these reluctantly rejected examples.

The essays follow the same general approach and are intended to explain how the Ontario countryside came to assume its characteristic appearance, and to answer some questions which may be suggested by the plates. They are not intended to give a complete account of the spread of settlement in Upper Canada, of the succession of styles in building, or of the development of farm practices. Such subjects are touched on because they affect the general picture, and are discussed in considerable detail when the details seem interesting in themselves and likely to be unfamiliar to some readers.

The facts set down and the conclusions drawn from them are the results of a good many years of research by the writer. In practically every case they can be documented from original sources, sometimes unpublished, or from reliable secondary sources. It seemed, however, undesirable to burden a text of this kind with an elaborate apparatus of documentation, and no notes simply citing sources have been included.

This book is very much of a joint effort. It is, in fact, nearly impossible to disentangle the separate parts played by the writer and the photographer in preparing this book for publication, and we both share the responsibility for it.

VBB & RG

Rural Ontario

The pattern

The pattern of rural landscape that inspired the making of this book came into being almost a century ago. By 1870 certain parts of Ontario had been settled for ninety-seven years, and almost all the southern part of the province for more than twenty. The process of clearing the land was not yet complete, but it was nearing completion. The lumbermen had long since begun to withdraw northward and westward in search of the magnificent trees which they considered the only ones worth cutting. In another ten years it would prove worthwhile to lumber what was left of the trees rejected in the 1860s and also the second growth that had come to maturity in some areas.

The main travelled roads no longer ran through long stretches of woodland – 'Long Woods', 'Seven-mile Woods', or 'Five-mile Woods'. Along the roads, the front fields of the farms were not only cleared and fenced but free from stumps. It was no longer the rule for farmers to clear a new 'wheat piece' every year. The average of cleared land on the farms was now about 55 per cent, and some farmers had hardly left themselves a sufficient woodlot. In fact, the chief differences noticeable between the rural landscapes of 1868 and of 1968 would be the prevalence of rail fences and the absence of trees in the earlier landscape. Except in a few regions, the settlers had spared none of the forest trees and they had not yet begun to plant shade trees, though many had set out orchards. Some bushes and small trees were beginning to grow along the fences, but the windbreaks and road avenues came later.

The great days of wheat-growing in this province had already passed by 1870, though it is probable that few farmers yet realized it. From the mid-1830s to the late 1860s wheat had, in spite of periods of lower prices, been a highly profitable crop; but in 1869 the price of wheat at Toronto dropped heavily to $1.00 a bushel. The prairie states had been productive for some years, and during the 1870s this competition was being felt; nevertheless peak prices were sometimes reached in the seventies and the price of Ontario wheat continued to fluctuate considerably up to 1883. By that time the Canadian prairies were being opened up and were producing wheat in quantity, and during the last decades of the century Manitoba wheat usually fetched a higher price at Toronto than wheat grown in Ontario.

These forty or so years of 'wheating' have left their mark on the Ontario country-side. Not only did they encourage the clearing of land and the building of better and larger barns, but it was with the cash from the sale of wheat that the log houses of the earlier days were replaced with others of frame, brick, or stone. The process began in the 1830s, but the great wave of building came between 1845 and 1865. A large proportion of the farmhouses of central Ontario and eastern Ontario date from these years. The proportion becomes lower as we go westward, but it is still considerable and, even west of London, houses of this period are fairly numerous and the proportion built before 1875 is high. This 'building boom' is reflected not only in the surviving examples but also in directories of the 1850s. These list in almost every town and village a remarkable number of builders, bricklayers, masons, and carpenters – far more than were required by the needs of the places concerned, though these also were largely being built at the time. Inns and stores were also built in considerable numbers. The School Act of 1846 and the Municipal Act of 1849 produced crops of schools and halls, and there was a good deal of building and rebuilding of churches, though perhaps rather more buildings of these types date from the years following Confederation.

There were, of course, changes after 1870. Methods of farming began to change after the coming of the cheese factories in 1866. The average number of cattle kept on the farms rapidly increased and the dependence on grain was lessened. When the 'cheese mania' began to moderate in the 1870s, farmers turned to the breeding for export of beef cattle, hogs, and horses. This meant larger stables and larger barns to store great quantities of hay and bedding straw. The surplus hay and straw could be sold to supply the multitude of teams, which formed the only transport on the roads and on the streets of the growing towns and cities.

More land was now in hay meadow or fenced pasture, and more and more farmers were using a regular rotation covering a number of years. This meant that the farm had to be divided up into a number of permanent fields, the use of which could be regularly changed. Square fields of ten to twelve acres had long been the norm, replacing both the great areas of wheat, sometimes mentioned in earlier periods, and the little 'pieces' which the pioneer had chopped out of the bush and thrown together or divided at will by moving his snake fences. Wire fencing was soon to make these fields more permanent than ever and the patchwork pattern of the farms became fixed.

The last third of the nineteenth century was not an altogether easy time for Ontario farmers. There were depressions in the mid-1870s and again in the 1890s, with a period of 'dull business' through much of the 1880s. In many Ontario townships rural population had begun to decline by 1871 and in others this decline began in the seventies or eighties. Some people were moving to the towns, where industry was expanding; others were going to the United States, especially to the prairies and the cities of the Middle West. By the mid-seventies the Canadian prairies began to attract farmers from Ontario (notably from Bruce County) and this movement was accelerated by the building of the Canadian Pacific Railway. The loss was not made up by immigration, which had greatly fallen off. In certain areas its chief effect was to remove most of the available farm labour; in others, farms were abandoned and either added to adjoining farms or, in some cases, left vacant to be used only for rough pasture. The abandoned farmsteads became in some sections a noticeable feature of the countryside.

Between the periods of difficulty there were, however, periods of prosperity, and the building, rebuilding, enlargement, and embellishment went on, though at a slower pace than formerly. This slow pace was not entirely due to hard times – many farms were already provided with a comfortable and roomy house which required very little in the way of modernization. More important to the farmers was the improvement of stock, of barns and fences, and the purchase of machinery to offset the shortage of labour. The great barns that are so characteristic of Ontario often date from the seventies or eighties, and it was in this period that the silo makes its appearance. The building and rebuilding of barns has never ceased and will not do so until new methods make the barn obsolete, an unlikely development in this climate.

The pattern of field, woodland, and road that covers the Ontario countryside grew gradually from the first small clearings, but it was not, as some may suppose, a haphazard growth, depending on the enterprise and choice of the individual settler. From the first, the government exercised a fairly rigid control over settlement and was, on the whole, successful in preventing random squatting. It is, therefore, futile to seek, as has sometimes been done, for a 'pattern of settlement' spontaneously following waterways or working consistently from one direction to another.

Private purchase from Indians was illegal; if the stories of such purchases have any truth in them, the purchaser was actually paying a kind of voluntary blackmail to be left undisturbed. In each story of this kind, the region in which the private sale is said to have taken place proves to have been regularly purchased from the Crown by treaty with some Indian nation, before the settler paid some cunning Indian a rifle, a white horse, or other picturesque consideration for his part of it. Further investigation also discloses a regular Crown grant of the holding, obtained in the normal way.

Once secured by the Crown, a 'purchase' was seldom opened for settlement until it had been surveyed into townships, and the townships divided into concessions and lots. There are some notable exceptions to this rule. In two important areas – at the Head of Lake Ontario and at Long Point – it is recorded that the Land Board of the District of Nassau in 1789–91 encouraged a number of settlers to establish themselves on unsurveyed land, on the understanding that after the survey they would receive grants to cover their improvements wherever possible. Such grants were duly made in both areas in 1795–96, when the surveys were far enough advanced to allow definite locations. It is stated that unauthorized squatters in the Long Point settlement (whose names are known in a few cases) withdrew from the area when the Acting Surveyor-General began his inquiry into the claims of the inhabitants. It is not known that any of them obtained legal title to land in Norfolk County.

Unauthorized squatting on Crown land was widespread in these early years, though the numbers of such squatters was probably not large. In 1794 the authorities took steps to control such squatting, apparently with a fair measure of success, for later squatters are chiefly heard of on unleased reserves or on unimproved private grants. There was, in the 1790s, a widely held belief that a 'right of soil' could be established simply by improving a vacant and unreserved lot. Surveyors reported that prominent settlers who had exhausted their own claims to Crown grants were 'improving' desirable lots by cutting a few trees and making a few piles of brush, and then selling their 'rights' to unsuspecting newcomers. When the latter eventually applied for confirmation of their title, they were sharply rebuked for being party to an illegal bargain and might be refused the desired grant, unless they had obviously acted in ignorant good faith and had resided long enough to have made further substantial improvements.

The notion that a right to land could be acquired by long occupancy had possibly some basis in common law, but more against private owners than against the Crown. To obtain such a right required, however, unchallenged use and possession for at least twenty years, hardly possible in Upper Canada before 1803 and not very likely to occur in any period. It does appear, however, that absentee owners and recipients of new Crown grants sometimes paid for improvements or for quit claim deeds to clear their title. Squatters on Crown or Clergy Reserves were often given the first chance to buy them when they came up for sale, and there are other cases where the government showed a sympathetic concern for squatters – for example when town plots were laid out on reserved land they had already occupied, as at Belleville and Woodstock. However, a lasting title to land was rarely obtained simply by squatting on it, and the great majority of land titles stem from a Crown grant obtained in the normal manner.

The method of obtaining a grant of land in Upper Canada did not affect the eventual appearance of the countryside, except in so far as it may have affected the pattern of survey. However, there seems to be a good deal of misunderstanding of this matter, and an explanation may be of interest, although it is a digression. The first step was for the intending settler to secure his right to a grant. This might always be done by petitioning the Governor-in-Council, but in the years following 1783 it was more usual to apply to local authorities – appointed agents (mostly commandants of forts) up to 1789, and after that the Land Boards of the four Districts – Lunenburg (at Cornwall), Mecklenburg (at Kingston), Nassau (at Niagara), and Hesse (at Detroit). The boards not only ordered the amount of land to which the applicant was entitled, but made definite locations, issuing 'certificates of occupation' by lot and concession.

After the division of the province of Quebec into Upper and Lower Canada in 1791, the first Lieutenant-Governor of Upper Canada, John Graves Simcoe, altered these arrangements in a way which increased the tendency to petition the Governor-in-Council. The majority of these petitions simply asked for land as a settler or as a privileged claimant, rarely mentioning either the quantity or a particular location. An order-in-council approving the grant would state the quantity of land, but usually left the location open. When a particular quantity of land was prayed for, the order sometimes gave less than was asked. When a particular location was mentioned, it was often approved, but there are many cases when it was refused, as, for example, applications for land 'at Long Point' which are frequently endorsed 'anywhere but at Long Point'.

The applicant was given a 'warrant of survey' stating the amount of his grant. He might then take this to the Surveyor-General's office to discover where there was a vacant lot more or less to his liking. His choice was then entered on the plan of the township and in the record book, and he was given a 'certificate of occupation' (later a 'location ticket'). Many settlers took lots which they had never seen, and were sometimes disappointed with what they found. If a lot was considered unfit for cultivation, it was sometimes exchanged for another vacant lot. Drawing for land is often mentioned in accounts of early settlement. It is true that the first Loyalists drew for their lots in the early 1780s, but this is very rarely referred to in the documents after 1789. When the Executive Council recommended drawing for lots on the new Dundas Street (Highway 5) in 1806, they treated it as a new departure and suggested details of procedure. Survey contractors, after 1819, drew for the land paid them for surveys. It does not appear that it was usual to make other grantees do so.

If the grantee decided he had found the lot on which he intended to settle, he would now begin the improvements which constituted his 'settlement duty' and entitled him to confirmation of his grant. Settlement duty is not clearly laid down before 1798, but it seems to have been understood that the building of a house and the clearing of some land were implied in the licence to 'occupy and improve'. Gradually the terms were made more specific. Grantees along Simcoe's military highways, Yonge Street and Dundas Street, were warned that they must build a house 20′ by 16′ 'in the clear' and have it occupied by a family within a year of the date of their grant. A little later a clearing of a certain size seems to have been demanded on Yonge Street, as well as the chopping, brushing, and burning of half the road allowance (33′) in front of their holding.

In 1798 these duties were extended to all settlers. They were to build a 20′ by 16′ house within a year, to occupy it in person or by deputy for a year, and within two years to clear, fence, and plant five acres and complete their road work. With some changes these duties continued to be demanded at least until 1830, and somewhat similar duties were required of free-grant settlers after that date. When the settler had procured a certificate sworn to by two persons that his duty had been performed, he could have his grant confirmed and was reasonably secure in possession. Many owners were content with this security and put off patenting. Land sometimes passed through five or six hands by sale or inheritance before the patent was finally issued, sometimes as long as thirty years after the original grant.

Delay in patenting was quite often due to reluctance to pay the survey and patent fees. All grants were nominally 'free', but all grantees had to pay for a survey of their holdings at a flat rate fixed according to acreage, and only privileged claimants got their patents gratis. These fees were small; in 1798 the survey fee was set at £1 7*s*. 6*d*. Halifax Currency (about $5.50 in silver) for 200 acres and the patent fee at sixpence Currency (10 cents) per acre. This was a cheap rate, but the high value of money at the time made it something more than a nominal one. It was quite sufficient to make many people put off payment until they had an urgent reason for doing so.

Prompt payment of fees was important to government, for this revenue was expected to meet the cost of specific services. The survey fees had been allotted to the expenses of the survey department and, if paid regularly, should have brought in a useful revenue. The amount of the patent fees was reduced by the great number of grants to privileged claimants – United Empire Loyalists, their children, Military Claimants, and others. A part of the patent fee was shared among about six officials, almost all of whom had a part in the complicated business of issuing a patent, as a perquisite of their office. Though the individual amounts were small, the total due to an officer might be as great or greater than his inadequate salary. When land fees fell badly in arrear, all the land officers, from the Lieutenant-Governor down, were out of pocket.

Privileged claimants tended to patent more promptly, since they paid no patent fee and were not expected to perform settlement duty on all their grants. Some, however, held their 'scrip', without locating a holding, until they had a chance to sell their rights to advantage. Even in the 1830s buying U.E. rights was a common way of obtaining land. These transactions were illegal, for scrip was not transferable; but it was easy to have the chosen lot granted to the holder of the warrant and then transferred to the purchaser by a proper assignment. Before 1800, however, free patents accumulated in the Provincial Secretary's office, increasing his expenses without bringing in money to cover them. Secretary William Jarvis complained in 1798 that his fees did not cover the cost of parchment and wax needed to engross and seal the deeds.

Lieutenant-General Peter Hunter, the second Lieutenant-Governor of Upper Canada, established a rule that fees were to be paid within two days of the date of the grant. This settled the question of arrears and removed one of the reasons for delay in applying for patents. He also exerted himself to prevent delay in the various offices through which the patent had to pass, and to see that ordinary settlers who had paid their fees got their patents promptly. This caused him to be accused of being greedy for fees, which seems to have been a slander, for in a contemporary letter he is stated to have renounced his share of the patent fee.* Hunter was also able to institute a new set of regulations – the 'regulations of 1804' – by which the fees were appreciably increased. These regulations remained in effect for about fifteen years, but the rule regarding payment caused so much complaint that it had to be withdrawn by his successor, Francis Gore. It is noticeable that a good many patents were issued during Hunter's term of office (1799–1805).

A large number of grants were made under the regulations of 1804, and many of these were not patented until some years later. The deeds issued for these patents have 'Reg. 1804' in the upper left-hand corner. This is the most conspicuous date on the deed, the others being in words in the text. It is often taken for the date of the grant, and it is sometimes nearly impossible to persuade the owner that the true date of the instrument is the one found in the last lines of the text – the date on which it was signed by the Lieutenant-Governor or Administrator. The actual grant will, of course, fall between January 1804 and January 1, 1819, when new regulations came in force.

When a grantee finally wished to obtain his deed, he had to produce proof that he had performed his settlement duty and taken the oath of allegiance before a magis-

* William Chewett & Thomas Ridout to D. W. Smith, Acting Surveyor-General, during his first trip (1799–1800) to England. Gore in 1812 succeeded in obtaining an allowance of £1,000 in lieu of land fees.

trate. He had then to see that a description of his land by 'metes and bounds' was properly made out at the Surveyor-General's office, and started on its way through the various offices where the deed was drawn up, signed, sealed, registered, and so forth. Finally a notice appeared in the *Gazette* that his deed, among others, was ready at the Secretary's office and might be called for. He now had a clear title to his freehold, could dispose of it as he saw fit, and was qualified to vote as a freeholder.

The system described applies best to the years 1794 to 1815, though it remained basically the same until an entirely different system was approved in 1827. Even in the early period there were certain exceptions, the most notable being the Talbot Settlement. Colonel Thomas Talbot for more than thirty years after 1804 acted as land agent for a constantly expanding area, which in the end more or less affected about twenty-nine townships. He had his own rather summary methods which omitted the first stages of normal process.

A number of details were changed after 1816, making the general system more complicated and increasing the fees. These changes aimed chiefly at checking impostures, producing more revenue, and enforcing settlement duty. New regulations with an increased scale of fees became effective on January 1, 1819, and exactly a year later a much higher scale was adopted to offset a provision for free grants of fifty acres to indigent immigrants. The regulations of January 1820 proved unsatisfactory. It was objected that the fees now amounted to a substantial purchase price, that most settlers needed more than fifty acres, and that many who could not pay the new fees were unwilling to declare themselves indigent. In 1824 the scale of 1819 was reintroduced. Already a different scheme was being discussed. The authorities were anxious to be free of the annoyances arising from the system of 'free grants'. The Crown Reserves in the surveyed townships were disposed of in 1826, the greater part being sold to the Canada Company, specially formed in Britain for this purpose. The Company had also been sold a huge unsurveyed tract, recently purchased from the Indians, when its attempt to buy the Clergy Reserves failed.

Under the new scheme introduced in 1827 unprivileged persons would normally buy Crown lands at auction, paying for them in four instalments over three years. Purchasers of small means were allowed to take land on a rental-purchase scheme and could buy up to 200 acres between auctions. The old privileged groups continued to receive free grants and a few new categories were added, such as the commuted military pensioners. Later free grants were made along a number of 'colonization' roads, but the normal way of obtaining land was by purchase from then on.

When it had become necessary in 1783–84 to assign lands to the settlers, chiefly Loyalists, who were entering the western parts of the province of Quebec, a form of subdivision was adopted that was, in spite of many variations, to be the basis of land division for more than a century. Lands purchased from the Indians were laid out in fairly large rectangular blocks, called at first 'seigniories'. This name was strongly objected to by the Loyalists and had to be changed to 'township'. The first townships were all on the shores of rivers or lakes and, except where local conditions caused variation, the approved form seems from the first to have been an oblong, appreciably longer than wide, with the length running back from the shore. Each township was divided into ranges of farm lots, which came to be called 'concessions' running across its width. An allowance for a road was usually provided in front of each concession, or every second concession, and along the boundary lines, and side roads occur at equal distances running straight through the length of the township.

In February 1789, the 'Rules and Regulation for the Conduct of the Land Department' standardized the form of townships, and plans were drawn up to illustrate a town and a township 'of Nine Miles front by Twelve Miles Depth' on a river or lake, and for a town and a township ten miles square, 'proposed for an Inland Situation'. The first is very much as described, except that the town, with its mile-square townplot, its belt of commons on three sides and its wider belt of small 'town farms' (also called 'park lots'), takes up half the front along the shore. The township has fourteen ranges of normal farm lots, with a road every second concession, twenty-four lots in each range and side roads at every six lots. The inland town is ten concessions deep, with thirty lots in each. The town with its belts of small holdings is in the centre. A map of 1790 shows the area between the Ottawa and the St. Lawrence divided into townships of this kind, almost all with their towns properly placed, and a township at 'Toronto' with its town fronting on the bay. Actually only three or four such towns were even partly laid out on the ground and in only one, Cornwall, was the mile-square plot completely surveyed. This solitary example survives as the plan of the older part of that city.

The oblong township, intended for the shore of a river or lake, became the type most often used before 1812. The square township was much rarer, even in 'an Inland Situation'. Local conditions continued to produce variations, but, apart from this, details varied from one group of townships to another. There might be changes in size and proportion, in the number of concessions, of lots in each concession, and in the width and depth of the lot. In a range of townships surveyed in 1791 between the River Trent and the 'Toronto Purchase',* the lots are normally a quarter of a mile wide, making the concessions $1\frac{1}{4}$ miles deep to give the required 200 acres. There is a road allowance in front of each concession and a side road every half mile. In the first survey of York Township (the front of the Toronto Purchase) the same size was used for ordinary farm lots, but the side roads come at every fifth lot, forming with the concessions a square of five lots or 1,000 acres. Most of the lots in this first survey run north and south, but in the Second and Third Concessions 'from the Bay' there were ranges of lots fronting 'on the Don', that is, on an allowance for a road which ran in theory straight up the valley from the front of Conc. I (Queen Street) and ended at the rear of Conc. III (on Eglinton Avenue). In Conc. III from the Bay this road is now Bayview Avenue. There was a similar range of east-west lots in these concessions 'on the Humber'.

The survey of York Township had only reached 'the road allowance in front of the

* The Toronto Purchase was a block of land running north from the shore of Lake Ontario and intended to include the northern end of the 'Toronto Portage' on the Holland River in King Township. Part of the eastern boundary still divides Scarborough from East York Township, while the western boundary now separates York and Peel Counties. When the purchase treaty was negotiated with the Mississaugas in 1784, it was believed that the purchase reached and crossed the Holland River; after survey this proved not to be the case, and a later treaty in 1798 was needed to extend the purchase.

Fourth Concession' when the decision in the autumn of 1793 to survey a highroad from Lake Simcoe changed the whole layout. Instead of continuing with east-west concessions 'from the Bay', concessions were surveyed east and west of Yonge Street and numbered from it. The concession roads are parallel to Yonge Street, but the sidelines of the lots were made parallel to the older concessions from the Bay, so that no roads meet at right-angles. Lots number northwards from Eglinton Avenue, and after Lot 25 new townships begin, fronting on Yonge Street; the lots in their first concessions (on Yonge Street) number consecutively from 26 well into the hundreds, while the other concessions start with one at the townline and end in normal fashion at the north boundary of the township.

Simcoe's Dundas Street (Governor's Road) was surveyed from Coote's Paradise (Dundas) to the Thames at the site of Woodstock earlier in 1793 and opened as far as the Grand River that autumn. It also had a series of townships fronting towards its line, both east and west of the Indian Lands, though here there was no continuous numbering. The practice of basing townships on a main road or special 'proof line' was continued later, but the road or proof line was not always made the 'baseline' or front concession road. It might have concessions on either side of it, like the 'Centre Road' through Toronto, Chinguacousy, and Caledon Townships, or even be a side road. As a rule the 'settlement' roads on which townships were based were kept as straight as possible and the concession lines did not deviate if this could be avoided. There were exceptions, even in the early period, like Bayham and Middleton Townships, where concessions follow the zigzags of the Talbot Road (1809–10). After 1840 the colonization roads, with their concessions of special-sized lots, were usually laid out without regard for the township surveys and cut drastically across the regular grid.

After 1816 it seems to have been felt that 100 acres made a better basic grant than 200 acres. This led to some experimentation with the form of survey, evidently directed at producing 100-acre lots with wider frontage and less depth, and later at reducing the number of road allowances. A slightly different scheme would be tried, used for a number of townships, and then changed again. These variations went on until the turn of the century, by which time most of the south-east part of the province was finally surveyed. However, the basis of all these schemes continued to be a rectangular grid of straight allowances for roads, although, as the surveys moved further north, it became increasingly difficult to make the actual roads conform to the grid.

This rigid grid is one of the chief characteristics of the Ontario countryside. It produces those long, straight roads that are seen extending into the distance across levels, or, from a high hill, dipping sharply to a valley and then appearing and disappearing for miles ahead as they cross the ridges. Such roads are usually concession lines, for side roads are likely to jog more or less, sometimes at each concession, for no reason easily apparent to the uninformed. The answer often lies in faults in chaining, not an easy task in heavy bush and, as was often the case, in winter weather. It was a common custom to chain along the front of one concession, marking the lots and the allowances for side roads, and then run up the townline to mark the rear corner, lay off the road allowance, and return along the front of the next concession marking lots and road allowances. A mistake on either line would spoil the correspondence of lot lines and side roads. The error might not be found until the individual lots were surveyed, and it might then be too late to correct it if some lots were occupied.

This grid of roads and lot lines lessened the work of survey, of land granting, and later of conveyancing. When it came to making roads in the early days of settlement, it was less satisfactory. Straight roads were all very well where the land was reasonably level, but much of Upper Canada was rolling country, and where level stretches of some size were found they were interrupted by swamps, 'slews', and ponds, and often cut by the deep valleys of large streams. The straight road allowances ran right across these, and in rolling country they climbed ridges and isolated hills without regard for the steepness of grades. With the primitive means of road-building available, to attempt to disregard such obstacles meant a prohibitive expense. A finished waggon road was, in any case, nothing more than a dirt track, with a slight attempt to ditch the sides and crown up the centre with the plough. There might be some crude terracing along hillsides; wet places were 'causewayed' with log corduroy; but grading of hills was kept to a minimum. It was both quicker and cheaper to go around a swamp or a steep hill, if this was possible. It was many years before the difficulties of bridging larger streams were overcome.

It is not much wonder, then, that many of the first roads were laid out 'cross lots' in 'Yankee' fashion, sometimes following an Indian path. These 'given' roads were once very numerous in the older parts of the province and are still often found east of Kingston. Because they crossed private property they were liable to be changed or closed at the will of the owner, unless they had been regularly established as legal roads on which statute labour could be demanded. At first such roads were established by request to the magistrates in Quarter Sessions, when a special jury was sometimes impanelled to decide the matter. Later a petition, signed by twelve inhabitants, to the District Road Commissioners would bring an order to the Supervisor of Roads or the Surveyor to inspect the road and report on a suitable line. Very often the line suggested would involve considerable straightening to interfere less with the layout of fields. Still later, when the surveyed roads had been improved, the given road might pass wholly or partly out of use. In many cases it has also passed out of memory, and is only recorded in an old 'road description' or surveyor's report.

The grid of roads also determined the layout of the farms and the fields into which they are divided. It fixed the pattern of field and fencerow which covers much of Ontario with little regard for natural features. There are a few places where the grid is lacking, notably in some of the large tracts bought or leased from the Iroquois of the Grand River. These lands had been purchased from the Mississauga by the Crown and granted to the Six Nations in 1784. The Crown reluctantly conceded the Indians' right to sell several large blocks and to lease others for 999 years. Later these tracts were laid out by their owners, some of whom followed the normal method. The 'German Company' in Waterloo Township laid out rectangular farms in regular ranges, but made no allowance for roads, which were formed later where they were needed. A tract along Fairchild's Creek east of Brantford, composed of individual leaseholds, is even more irregular, the shape of the farms and the course of the roads being largely determined by the many windings of the creek.

The buildings

The type of log construction used by the first settlers in Ontario had been foreign to the British colonists in North America. It is believed to have been introduced by the Swedish settlers in Delaware, though some of the Germans who settled in Pennsylvania may have been acquainted with this method in Europe. It was not until the eighteenth century that the British colonists began to use it for dwellings, and then chiefly in recently occupied frontier areas. By the outbreak of the revolution in 1774 log houses had become the rule on the frontiers.

The French in Canada also used this method of building by laying up logs to form cribs (*pièce sur pièce*), especially for rough cabins, for outbuildings and for fortifications, but they normally preferred a method they had brought from France, in which shorter pieces of dressed timbers were morticed into the grooved uprights of a stout timber frame. This was called *entre poteaux* or *en colombage*.

The Loyalists who flocked into 'the upper parts' of the old province of Quebec in 1783–89 were familiar with the idea of log dwellings, even if some had never seen any. Of necessity almost all of them built round-log 'houses', 'cottages', or 'huts' as soon as they were allowed to go to their lands. The term 'log cabin' was not in general use at this time; it is rarely found before 1800. The first houses were probably small and roughly built, for their builders hoped to replace them as soon as possible. The list of tools requested by the Loyalists assembled at Cataraqui (Kingston) shows that they hoped to be able to build houses of fair size, well finished and well lighted, for each settler was to receive a remarkably large number of window panes in two sizes. The government could not meet these requests in full, even had it been willing to do so, and the Loyalists had to be content with more modest equipment and housing. Nevertheless, other tools besides axes were issued, and several government sawmills were built to provide plank and boards. Within ten years a good many settlers had been able to build better houses. Mrs Simcoe noted that in her walks around Kingston it was pleasant to see the new houses with the old cabins standing beside them.

Not all the buildings put up in the first years of settlement were log. The government, with military and naval artificers at command, was apt to build in frame. The government grist mills seem to have been frame buildings, and there was a frame store-house, beside the mill on the Four-Mile Creek near Niagara, which was moved after 1790 to Palatine Hill to become part of the Servos house. A frame church was built in 1785 for the Mohawks of the Grand River and still stands, somewhat altered, at Brantford. There were skilled artisans among the refugees, in addition to those brought from the French settlements. Some settlers were able to build better buildings at once. Examples are the Elliott house near Amherstburg and the modest house built about 1786 for Sir John Johnson at Williamstown in Glengarry County. The Elliott house was frame covered with clapboard, but Sir John's house, now the wing of a later building, is of dressed timber *entre poteaux*, a method not often used in this province.

We know little of the appearance of the better buildings built before 1789. Only one or two have survived and none has survived unaltered. They may have been 'neat and even elegant', as the Reverend Mr Stuart wrote of some in Kingston, but they were modest in size and architectural pretensions. Between 1789 and 1799 a number of more important houses were built, as well as some churches and a few public buildings. Many of these buildings have perished, but we know what they looked like, thanks very largely to Mrs Simcoe's habit of sketching. Others survived long enough to be photographed and a few are still standing. The number of these survivors is probably not so many as is supposed by some people. There has been a tendency (common enough elsewhere) to push back the date of old houses, and these datings have not always stood up to careful investigation. In many other cases the early date is quite unsupported by any reliable evidence and the probabilities are against it.

Such confusion in dating is well illustrated by the tradition that has often been accepted concerning the stone house in Wellington, Prince Edward County, called 'The Manor'. This has it that the house was built in 1769 'by the Indians' for Daniel Reynolds, a fur trader, and that 'Lady' Simcoe was ill there for two weeks. This remarkable story has been traced back a little more than seventy years, but no further. It seems to be an imaginative expansion of a statement in the *Historical Atlas of Hastings and Prince Edward Counties* (1878) that Daniel Reynolds, a Loyalist, was the first settler on the site of Wellington and lived for some time 'among the Indians' before other settlers arrived. The writer cautiously remarks that the date of Reynolds's settlement was not certainly known.

The tale of 'Lady' Simcoe's illness is, of course, a complete error – a confused recollection of the fact that Mrs Simcoe was ill for five or six days at Johnstown, a little east of Prescott, on her return trip from Quebec in February 1795. She was never nearer to Wellington than the Bay of Quinte, and her diary shows that the party did not enter Prince Edward County. This mistake would be enough to cast doubt on the other statements, if they were not, in themselves, so unlikely as to be incredible. Without some contemporary evidence, which is entirely lacking, it is impossible to believe that an unmarried trader would go to the trouble of building himself a stone house in an untouched wilderness, especially as this would draw attention to the fact that, contrary to regulations, he was not trading at one of the forts – an offence that could cause the confiscation of his goods. That he could build such a house with only Indians to help him is nearly as difficult to accept.

It is just possible that, when the address in which this erroneous account was first given to the public was printed in a local newspaper, a misprint occurred of '1769' for '1789'. The latter date is not at all improbable for the beginning of the building. Such a house might well take two or three years to finish and may have been ready for occupation only a short time before April 30, 1792, when 'Daniel Reynolds, Ameliasburg, bachelor . . .' was married by the Reverend John Langhorn to 'Nancy Waight, Sophiasburg, spinster'. Even this date, 1789–91, leaves the Manor among the very small number of buildings surviving from before 1800 and the still smaller number from before 1795. It is certainly one of the oldest stone houses in the province and one of the most interesting, though some details of the exterior may date from a renewal about ninety years ago.

Investigation of some other cases has reduced the number of survivors from the eighteenth century. Among these is the James Baby house at Sandwich (now part of the city of Windsor); this used to be dated to 1790 and even called 'the first brick house in Ontario'. It should have taken very little research to reveal that the townplot of Sandwich was laid out by the Crown and the town lots distributed in 1797, that the surveyor's plan of 1797 shows no house in the townplot, although a windmill, two farmhouses, and a church are shown near it, and that the Hon. James Baby did not get his deed to the lot on the corner of Russell and Mill Streets (No. 5), on which the house stands, until 1807. Some of this information was printed in 1931 and other documents were published in 1960, but they all have been easily available for many years. The James Baby house, therefore, belongs in the 1801–12 group, and may be no older than the house built by Francis Baby, the younger brother of James, on the site of the later town of Windsor.

In another instance the discovery of unpublished documents has confirmed suspicions about the early date given to the large frame house built by Joseph Brant on the site of Burlington. These arose from examination of the history of the 'Brant Tract' and were strengthened by the fact that Mrs Simcoe does not mention this house in her diary. Some letters of Brant in the Nelles Papers in the Ontario Archives show him to have been planning the house soon after receiving confirmation of his grant in 1798 and ordering lumber for it from Robert Nelles of 'The Forty' (Grimsby). The house seems to have been built about 1800–01 and Brant paid for the lumber in 1802.

Apart from the need for historical accuracy, the exact dating of buildings, where possible, is of importance in the matter of style. If Brant House had really been built about 1785, it would be by far the most ambitious building of that decade whose appearance has been recorded in some detail. The James Baby house has been cited as an example of an eighteenth century house, and its features discussed as if they belonged to 1790. On the other hand there has been a tendency to date Poplar Hall near Maitland (PLATE 6) *after* 1812; but the assessment roll for Augusta Township shows that William Wells was taxed in 1812 on a house very like Poplar Hall, and seems to confirm the statement in the older county history that he was taken prisoner by the Americans in the existing house during the war of 1812–14.

Almost no log buildings have survived from before 1800. An exception is the Scadding cabin, now in the grounds of the Canadian National Exhibition at Toronto. This was built on John Scadding's farm on the east bank of the Don in 1796 to replace a larger log house burned a little before. It is very close to the size – 16′ by 20′ in the clear – required as a minimum from all settlers on Yonge Street and Dundas Street at that time. A squared-timber house in Markham may date to 1800; it is not mentioned in a report of 1798. Mrs Simcoe's sketches of log and timber houses show that they resembled those built at a much later date, and the ones included in this collection give a good idea of their appearance after improvement had taken place.

A larger number of frame houses have survived; but frame buildings are easy to alter and only a few are in anything like their original condition. Most have been moved, resheeted or enclosed in additions, until little more than the frame, parts of the chimney stacks, or some remnant of the plan remains of the older house. In many cases these changes took place more than a century ago and the house may still possess a good deal of interest. In others the mishandling has been more recent and even more drastic and has sometimes been due to well-intentioned but ill-informed attempts at 'restoration'.

From the few survivors and the pictorial evidence we can form some idea of the fashion in building prevailing in the 1790s. The various houses have certain features in common, which can be traced to the 'Georgian' style of the old colonies in the mid-eighteenth century, but which were beginning to be outmoded there by 1774 and were definitely so in the United States in the 1790s. This lag in style might be expected, for settlers in a new country seldom imitate the most recent fashions in the land they have left, but rather those which are at the same time familiar and reasonably modern in appearance. In most cases neither the builders nor their clients would yet possess the latest architectural books, from which details in the new manner might be drawn. The craftsmen, whether Loyalist, 'Yankee', or French, would follow the rules they had been taught in their youth, guided by the taste of their employers.

The most conspicuous feature characterizing these early houses was the emphasis on a high, steep-pitched roof, usually kept free of dormers, at least in front, though sometimes broken by a central gable, low and broad enough to suggest a pediment. Such roofs had been a feature of colonial 'Georgian' in the 1730s, '40s, and '50s, but were already being reduced in height before 1770. Almost all the houses sketched by Mrs Simcoe have these high roofs and they appear in the Fairfield house – The White House – near Millhaven (1793), the brick Meyers house at Belleville, and the stone Cartwright house at Kingston. The last two have been destroyed but are known from old photographs. The Cartwright house had dormer windows, and would not have looked out of place in Montreal. This raises the question of how far these lofty roofs may have been due to the influence of French builders. It is recorded that artificers from Montreal, as well as from Niagara, were sent to Fort Frontenac in 1783, and that French contractors were working in Grenville County in 1800, when Homewood, a stone house still standing near Maitland, was built by Louis Brillière for Dr Solomon Jones. It is notable that high, steep roofs continued to be built in the eastern part of the province long after a lower, flatter type had become the rule west of Kingston.

There were probably French Canadians working on buildings at York in the 1790s, for Mrs Simcoe's diary and sketches make it clear that Castle Frank was built *entre poteaux* in the French manner. This, however, is an isolated instance; none of the known names of contractors working in York at this period are French. Other features of these early houses can be paralleled in Lower Canada, but are common to both the French and English colonies. It is likely that the details of design would, in any case, be dictated by the client rather than by the contractor or craftsmen. French-Canadian craftsmen were by this time accustomed to working for employers of British origin; they had learnt to produce work in 'the English taste' and the influence of this taste could already be discerned in the architecture of Lower Canada. Soon houses entirely in the 'English' manner were to be built there in fair numbers, among them one built for the Hon. François Bâby of Montreal at St. Pierre-des-Becquets, which is remarkably like the two built for his cousins beside the Detroit River in Upper Canada.

Another feature of these early houses is the simple treatment of the entrance doorway. All those pictured in contemporary drawings have doorways without side-lights, often with a small transom and only occasionally with a semicircular arch and fanlight. The doorway of the McFarland house (PLATE 7) illustrates the type very well. Possibly the first arched doorway appeared on the William Dickson house in Newark (Niagara-on-the-Lake). This house was burnt with the rest of the town in 1813, but Dickson attached an elevation of it to his claim for compensation. This shows a two-storeyed house, 50′ by 40′, that appears to be built of large blocks of dressed ashlar, but the drawing of Dickson's farmhouse (1811) has the walls treated in the same way, although the house is stated to have been brick. It is likely that the large house was also brick and was the one referred to in a petition of 1793. In this petition Dickson says he had 'built the first brick house in the province'.

Since the James Baby house must now be dated after 1801, the earliest doorway whose side-lights seem certainly to be original is the one at Homewood. The side-lights of the White House look as though they might be alterations made when the upper windows were cut down to form French doors. They are glazed with one normal pane and one narrow one on the outside, a manner of glazing fashionable after 1845, especially for side-lights and French windows. Such alterations are easy in frame houses, and are difficult to verify without a rather destructive examination.

These simple doorways were sometimes dignified by a small porch, usually with two columns supporting an entablature and pediment. Verandas were not unknown, but were rarely found on the larger houses. The White House near Millhaven is unique in having two storeys of galleries on its entrance front.* Robert Hamilton's stone house at Queenston had galleries 'above and below' on the river side, supported, it would appear from Mrs Simcoe's sketches, by square piers running from the ground to the eaves, like the colonnade added to Mount Vernon in 1787. It is curious to find such a feature in Upper Canada so soon after Washington introduced it into Virginia. Verandas or 'stoops' seem to have been slightly more common on smaller houses. Mrs Simcoe shows one across the front of Mrs Tice's frame house near Niagara Falls, and indicates one at the back of a house at Pointe-au-Baudet on the same page of her diary as her larger sketch of Glengarry House.

Glengarry House, whose tall, stone gable ends still stand near the St. Lawrence in Charlottenburgh Township, was not quite finished when the Simcoes dined with its

* It is not certain that the galleries on the south front of the Gage house at Stoney Creek are original. There is clear evidence that this house has been altered, the principal entrance having been moved from the north to the south front. Besides there seems to be some uncertainty as to the date of this house.

owner in 1792. Mrs Simcoe made a small outline sketch of the house beside the entry in her diary recording this visit. When she stopped there briefly on her way to Quebec in the autumn of 1794, she made a second larger sketch of 'Glengary House'. These drawings show that Colonel John MacDonell, Speaker of the Legislative Assembly and Lieutenant of Glengarry County among other offices, had dignified his mansion with certain features that enhanced its resemblance to lairds' houses built a generation earlier in his native Scotland, but which also occur in houses in Upper Canada before 1820. Over the plain doorway was one of those 'Venetian' windows, beloved of Palladians, in which the wide central light has a semicircular arch while the narrower side-lights have straight lintels. Above was a gable, a little steep-pitched for a pediment, pierced by a broad semicircular window; the pediment is flanked by dormers.

The Dickson house at Newark had a similar scheme of Palladian window and pediment, this time with a small round window. Here the whole composition, including a curious porch and an arched doorway, was projected slightly to form a central 'pavilion'. Brant House had a Palladian window above a pedimented porch with four slender columns, but no pediment in the roof. This was also the scheme used for the first brick dwelling in York (Toronto), built for Quetton St. George in 1810, though here the porch echoed the Palladian motif. Finally, the scheme of a true Palladian window with pediment and half-round window above was used in the Reverend John Strachan's house on Front Street in 1818. Soon after this, however, the true Palladian window with its round arch seems to have gone out of favour, though in the late twenties, the thirties, and forties three-light windows with a straight lintel or with an elliptical arch over all three lights are often found above doorways. About 1850 the round-arched Palladian window is again part of the builders' repertory and Gothic variations on the theme have become common. The central pediment in the roof continued to be used, especially in houses of one-and-a-half storeys, growing steadily steeper in pitch, until it lost all resemblance to a classical pediment and developed into the 'peak'.

There was no sudden change in style when the eighteenth century ended. Some builders and their employers continued to prefer the older fashions, but by 1800 there were already signs of an approaching change. The influence which caused this came chiefly from the United States. In the twenty years before 1812 much of the immigration into Upper Canada was from Vermont, New York, and Pennsylvania. There the manner of building fashionable after 1789 has been called the 'Federal' style. This was to a large extent derived from English work of the last third of the eighteenth century, the style that has been commonly, but not entirely correctly, called 'Adam'. The style of Robert Adam, his contemporaries, and his immediate successors is regarded as the beginning of Neo-classicism in England, and the style prevailing in Upper Canada from 1815 to 1830 has lately been called 'Neo-classic'.

This term is not entirely satisfactory; a layman is apt to be confused when he finds that it covers such diverse buildings as the Pantheon in Paris and an Upper Canadian farmhouse. His confusion may be deepened when he learns that the name covers also the Greek, Gothic, and late Regency modes which make their appearance in Upper Canada around 1830. The addition of 'Loyalist' to Neo-classic is open to objections, but, until some better term is agreed upon, it will at least serve to distinguish this phase from others which come later and to a large extent replace it.

There are not many indications of the Loyalist Neo-classic to be found in the houses built before 1812. One of the first signs of change is the abandonment of the high, steep roof, which is found in several examples, the McFarland house (PLATE 7) among them. The James Baby house at Sandwich, although most of its details follow the older fashion, has a round arched doorway with a fanlight, flanked by slender pilasters supporting a light entablature, and placed between side-lights treated as separate windows. This doorway has some resemblance to that of the William Wells house, Poplar Hall (PLATE 6), which is more elaborate. If the evidence of the assessment rolls is accepted, the latter must be dated to about 1811. Even externally it is very advanced in style for so early a date, and the interior is an even fuller example of this manner. Its fine details might suggest that the fitting-up had been carried out after the War of 1812. There is, however, no need to suppose this; there are other cases of individuals being ahead of the fashion, and these details could be derived from books published in America before 1806, such as the later works of William and James Pain and the first books by Asher Benjamin.

Another house 'built the year preceding the war', i.e. in 1811, was William Dickson's brick farmhouse. This is shown in a drawing attached to his claim for compensation as a one-storey cottage on a high basement. It had a veranda recessed between the ends of two narrow wings, and the low, hipped roof was carried across both wings and veranda. The doorway was arched, with a rayed fanlight, but it lacked pilasters or side-lights. It was, however, the pillars supporting the roof over the veranda that showed the most direct connection with the new mode. It is impossible to tell from the drawing what kind of capital is intended, but the slender shafts, tapered and slightly bulging, are marked with lines which almost certainly indicate convex reeding, spiralling around the column (spiral fluting is possible but much less likely). Attenuated half-columns with spiral reeding were often employed in 'New England Federal' to decorate doorways, certain windows, and mantelpieces. There are examples of this use in Ontario at Prescott and Grafton. I do not know of any other example of free-standing columns so decorated, but there may have been cases which did not survive. Certainly, spirally reeded pillars had no place among the details of the older 'Georgian' style.

The houses of this pre-war period conform in almost all cases to the shape which had been normal before the Revolution, and was to remain the rule until Confederation and after. They were oblong, with the entrance in a long side, and were usually symmetrical, with two windows evenly spaced on each side of the doorway, and five windows above in houses of two full storeys – what is called 'a five-bay front'. There were, of course, exceptions; Mrs Simcoe shows one or two asymmetrical houses with two windows on one side of the door and only one on the other. This four-bay type was to become common in the St. Lawrence townships, especially in Dundas County. Houses with only three openings appear in some other sketches, and occasionally an extra pair of full-sized windows would be placed on either side of the door to light a large hall, giving seven openings on a front. Nevertheless, five openings were usual on the front with a good many windows in the ends, in spite of the high cost of glass.

This multiplicity of windows very soon attracted the attention of British travellers accustomed to the effects of Pitt's window tax. The Earl of Selkirk, at York in January 1804, wrote: 'Some few houses are filled up with brick between the frame, but the generality not – & they have a number of cold windows – the seasons are not severe enough to make them attend to comfort.' Selkirk was a Scot, and North American windows probably struck him as large as well as numerous, for 'modern' windows of these proportions were still a fairly recent novelty in Scotland in modest buildings. The brick filling of the frame was rather more common in the St. Lawrence townships. It was a continuation of a New England practice and was due to the belief that unfilled frame houses were cold. This belief arose from the hasty building with unseasoned lumber, the form of clapboard then in use, and to some extent from the cost and scarcity of nails. Wide clapboards, partly seasoned, simply tapered and overlapped, and not sufficiently nailed down, were likely to warp and curl, letting cold into the air space which, if sealed, would have been better insulation than any of the fillings. Other fillings used (later at any rate) were sun-dried brick, plain clay, and a mortar-like cement.

Windows were fairly large, though rather smaller than they became later. The increase in size was due to the use of larger panes of glass. In 1804 panes 7″ by 9″ seem to have been usual for upper windows, lower ones might be 'larger size', perhaps 8″ by 10″ or 9″ by 11″. There were normally 24 panes to a window, twelve to each of the two sliding, double-hung sashes.* There were some variations; sometimes the upper sash in a window had four rows of four panes and the lower only two rows, or windows of an upper floor might be reduce in height with less than 24 panes. In an area including parts of Markham and Whitchurch Townships, some houses have sash with the old small panes but only three panes wide, with 18 or 21 panes in all, making the openings tall in proportion to their width. These houses may be as late as 1840.

John MacTaggart, another Scot, whose *Three Years in Canada* fell between 1825 and 1828, claimed that he could 'tell what nation the natives of the houses *hail from*' by the type of their dwelling. He describes 'the mansion of Jonathan, or the United Empire Loyalist from the United States': 'A house ... chiefly built of wood, and painted white, with nine windows and a door in front, seven windows in either gable, and a *semicircular* one above all, almost at the top angle of the roof, the blinds painted green, the chimney stalks highly ornamented, and also the fanlight at the door; the barns, stables, &c. off from the house at a great distance; the arches of all

* Window weights were a luxury rarely found in farmhouses then or 100 years later.

the shed-doors turned of wood in eccentric elliptics.' MacTaggart must have had a fairly new house in mind, one built after 1816 and a rather exceptional one at that. Four windows in the end walls were more common than six, and few houses can have had an ordinary window to light the attic with a semicircular one above it as he seems to imply. Half-round or half-oval windows often are found in the gables of two-storeyed houses, but they are usually the only ones. Rectangular windows in this position may be single or a pair; in the latter case they are often very small.

The Loyalist Neo-classic was very much the fashion from 1816 on and held the field until the later 1820s. By then new influences (equally Neo-classic, but not Loyalist) were beginning to be felt. Nevertheless, this style continued in use through the 1830s and into the 1840s, and belated examples can sometimes be found after 1860. It can often be found mixed with the newer modes, Regency, Greek, or Gothic. In Upper Canada it was to a great extent a builder's style, especially in the country. Except for a few important buildings, there is little evidence of design by professed architects.

The style seemed to some old-country observers to be over-elaborate and incorrect. MacTaggart, in the passage quoted, goes on to refer to 'a disposition to be showy and clean, without neatness, proportion or substantiality'. Another observer calls the 'Yankee's house' 'as gay as paint and plane can make it'. Certainly a considerable emphasis on ornament was characteristic, and this ornament had a smallness of scale more suitable for interiors than façades. It not infrequently seems that the joiner has been given a free hand and has trimmed the window over the front door like the frame of a parlour mirror, or has treated door and windows as if they were mantelpieces. In some cases, mostly interior work, the love of ornament is carried to excess and the elaboration becomes fussy and fantastic in a way that seems decidedly 'Late Victorian'. In fact, the excessive phase of the New England Federal appealed to some designers of the 1890s and was used in a coarsened form in some mantels and over-mantels.

As a rule, however, the Loyalist Neo-classic builders showed an admirable restraint, and their work has dignity as well as refinement. Incorrect their work certainly was, for they took extraordinary liberties with the rules for the classic orders. Columns and pilasters are usually too slender for their height; entablatures are compressed or expanded and, under the eaves, are rarely in the right proportion. The Greeks had occasionally used an oblong metope, just as they sometimes put a base on a Doric column, but the designer of Poplar Hall is unlikely to have known of the precedents. No Greek or any architect that I know of ever carried a triglyph frieze up the sides of a pediment under the raking cornices, as was done not only on the main pediment of the Barnum house but even on the little pediment over the doorway. To some extent these departures from rule derived from the practice of old-world architects of a generation or two earlier, but there had long since been a reaction and both theory and fashion had taken a different direction.

Until after the War of 1812 a great proportion of the inhabitants of Upper Canada were of North American origin. They, their parents, or their grandparents had come to the province from some other part of this continent, and the number of settlers from across the Atlantic was comparatively small. By 1816 the great movement of settlers from Britain had begun. The numbers were still few compared with those of the thirties and forties, but they were sufficient to have some influence on the life of the country, as the older settlers were well aware. If John MacTaggart is to be believed, they had already in the late 1820s begun to introduce a different way of building houses. He describes 'the dwelling of an honest English farmer' as 'a plain rectangular house of brick or stone, with five windows and a door in front, and a window, perhaps, in either gable'. He says that 'the wealthy Lowland Scotchman follows the same plan nearly'. This description, when compared to the account of the Loyalist's house, does bring out some of the differences of the type preferred by the recent immigrants – its plainness and the reduced number of windows. But it is strange that MacTaggart should have seen enough of such houses in the 1820s to consider them a special class, especially as he is describing a two-storeyed house.

A good many of the immigrants after 1816 had been farmers of substance, whether English, Scottish, or Irish. Some of these had bought improved farms in settled areas and so might be able to build a good house before 1827, but not many of these houses were of stone or brick and few would boast a full upper storey. Returns of assessment, sent to the Legislative Assembly by District Clerks between 1824 and 1850, show that houses of masonry were quite rare in many districts and, even where stone houses were more common, they were still far less numerous than they are now. The greater number of these 'taxable houses' were in the 'Frame, less than two stories' class. Dwellings of round logs, which still formed a majority, were not assessed at this period.

An act of the Upper Canada Legislature in 1803 made houses with two or more fireplaces in use subject to taxation. The form of assessment attached to the act divided such houses into 'Houses in Town' and 'Houses in the Country', with a column for 'Additional Fireplaces'. An act of 1807 introduced six categories, grading taxable houses according to kind of construction and number of storeys – 'Round Logs', 'Square Timber, one story', 'Square Timber two story', 'Framed under two story', 'Brick or stone of one story with not more than two fireplaces', 'Brick or stone of two story with not more than two fireplaces', each class having its column for additional fireplaces. Taverns were now dropped from the rolls. The lowest class, round-log houses, was omitted under the Act of 1811, which altered the definition of the next class to include timber hewn on two sides and 'houses one story and not two stories'. The fifth, or highest, class became 'Frame, brick or stone of 2 stories', an ambiguity inconvenient to future historians. This class seems to have been assessed at £150 (probably Provincial Currency, i.e. $600 in silver) and another £50 was added for each storey over two. This may not have been high compared to the cost of building a two-storied house in 1811*; but it was out of proportion to the assessment

* From actual tenders in York in 1804, a frame house 40′ by 30′, of two storeys, cellar and attic, with eight main rooms and at least four fireplaces in two chimney stacks, could be built for $2,500 to $2,700 Silver. About 1842, $500–700 could buy an acre town lot and build a house on it of about this size, and a frame farmhouse 40′ by 24′, probably of one and a half storeys, cost only about $250.

of the other classes which ranged from £20 to £40. In 1820, when building costs had probably fallen somewhat, the assessment for 'Frame, brick or stone of two stories' was reduced to £60, with £10 for each fireplace over two. Stoves counted as fireplaces for assessment. Otherwise the five classes remained the same for another thirty years.

There is no doubt that this method of assessment had some effect on the types of houses favoured in Upper Canada. It encouraged the use of round logs (usually dressed on the inside) for permanent dwellings in spite of some disadvantages of this type of construction and a widely held prejudice against it. By establishing what amounted to a hearth tax, it tended to limit the overall size of houses and to ensure that, in some cases, they were inadequately heated.* It also served to increase the popularity of the storey-and-a-half house, and to make it the usual type of farm dwelling in this province. A full upper storey increased the cost of construction, especially where the walls were of brick or stone, but this might not have offset the inconveniences of these early attics, scant of head room, inadequately lighted and ventilated, roasting hot in summer and, before stoves became common, often cold in winter. That these inconveniences were felt is clear from the tendency to heighten the walls to the eaves, to enlarge the gable windows as chimney flues became fewer and smaller, and to insert small windows under the eaves almost at the floor or larger ones in 'peaks'. However, the fact that a house of less than two storeys paid appreciably less tax than a house of two storeys with the same superficial area and the same number of rooms, and that this disparity increased with each additional fireplace, certainly influenced some settlers to decide to forgo the added comfort and superior status derived from possession of a house of two full storeys.

The practice of rating a neighbour's standing by the kind of house he inhabited must have derived in part from the method of assessment, for where it obtained it made use of all six original classes. Whether it was universal may be questioned, but in some areas it outlasted the old form of assessment abolished by the Act of 1853. Ernest Thompson Seton has twice given an amusing account of the working of this system near Lindsay in the early 1870s and of the consternation occasioned when a family suddenly exchanged a 'hogpen cabin', of round logs with untrimmed corners, for a fine brick house, without going through the proper stages of dressed timber, frame, and so forth. Probably this caste system was not always so clearly marked, but a handsome house would confer prestige on its owner, if he proved to have the means to maintain it.

The manner of building which the immigrants brought with them from the British Isles was a phase of the Regency style which had been applied in the old countries chiefly to minor buildings – to cottages, farmhouses, villas and, of course, to town houses built as speculations. It was marked by an increasingly plain treatment of exteriors, ornament being restricted to the principal doorway and perhaps the openings directly above it. Fewer and larger windows were used, and in masonry buildings the window frames were set back to give a reveal and were almost entirely concealed by the masonry. Doorways are likely to be more deeply recessed, the door with its

* It is not stated clearly in the acts that all houses with only one hearth were exempt from assessment, but there is reason to think that they were thus interpreted by some assessors.

side-lights and transom being in line with the inside of the wall, and the jambs and soffit of the opening panelled. In Upper Canada the 'Regency' designers did not reject the elliptical arch, which had already begun its long popularity which was to last into the 1860s. It was used for doorways and as an alternative to the round arch in windows above them, but there was a tendency to substitute a straight lintel in both positions. Successful design in this way of building depended almost entirely on a skilful control of proportions, with little assistance from 'paint and plane'. It was a practical style, and, in its time and place, a functional one. It could achieve a considerable degree of quiet elegance, but in its basic form made few concessions to the picturesque.

Examples of this new style begin to appear in the years before 1830, and some have survived. They show some degree of admixture with the earlier manner and this mixing was to continue. There was also mixture with other influences which appear in the 1830s – the 'Grecian' and the 'Picturesque', which latter in Upper Canada usually took the form of 'Gothic' at this time. The Grecian taste came to Upper Canada chiefly from the United States, where it was flourishing by 1830 and continued to flourish until the Civil War. This style never came to full flower in Canada, partly because the tall columns characteristic of it were too costly for most private builders, and partly because the more sophisticated immigrants, as their writings make clear, despised the Grecian mode. It had lately been fashionable in Britain, but was now less used for domestic work and was regarded as suitable only for large and monumental buildings. By the standards of these colonists there were almost no large houses in Upper Canada – the inhabitants lived in cottages or at most small villas. They thought it ridiculous and pretentious to decorate such small dwellings with the full panoply of classical columns, pilasters, entablatures, and window architraves, all the more if these followed the larger-scaled Greek orders and had to be executed in wood instead of stone or plastered brick. They were besides badly bitten with the rage for the picturesque, and considered that some form of picturesque cottage was usually most suitable to Canadian scenery – Gothic, Rustic, or perhaps 'Swiss'. An elegant villa in a simple classic style might be permitted in some situations, especially if it was rendered picturesque by being surrounded by verandas.

It was during the period of the great immigration in 1825–55 that the encircling veranda came into its own in Upper Canada. Hitherto this feature had been used sparingly, kept off the front and often off the main block altogether, limited to the side of wings and rear ells. Some houses built by well-to-do immigrants before 1830 are recorded to have had verandas on three sides and some had verandas across the back only. After 1830 examples become more and more common. The liking for the picturesque induced some colonists to seize on log-building as a native method from which a local style might be formed, and the group of fanciful log houses which resulted from this idea all involved verandas to a greater or less degree.

The veranda of a Regency house might extend only across the front and even be recessed between wings, but it was more characteristic for it to continue around one or both ends or even around the whole house. At first a plain, lean-to roof was used, often hipped at the ends, and supported by slender posts, only very rarely by columns. In log houses the rustic effect might be emphasized by using logs, with the bark on, for supports. More normal were neat piers of slight girth with capitals, neck-moulds, and bases, or the solid square posts used in the earlier fashion, chamfered at the corners to increase their slenderness and usually also supplied with mouldings to suggest capitals and bases (PLATE 24). The former usually supported a simplified architrave, but the latter often had a fascia board 'turned ... in eccentric elliptics' or some simple form of bracket. The more fantastic types of scrolled, fretsaw bracket come later and are usually combined with a heavier post. Not many of these earliest Regency verandas remain unchanged. They were very liable to decay, and did not appeal to succeeding generations. There was no easier way of modernizing a house than by giving it a new veranda in the latest fashion, and many Regency houses now have verandas of the sixties, seventies, and eighties.

Much more typically Regency were the verandas supported by some form of trellis work. Balconies and verandas with treillage supports had been popular in England from near the beginning of the nineteenth century. They were a town feature found on terraces as well as on villas, and particularly favoured in watering places, whether spas or seaside resorts. Very narrow and more often placed on an upper floor, they looked much more flimsy than the Upper Canadian version more or less solidly based on the ground. It seems possible that treillage was introduced in this province in the 1830s, but most examples are later than 1840, and it seems to have been particularly popular around 1850. The Thomson house (PLATE 25) was said by its owner in 1949 to be then a hundred years old. It is largely the veranda that gives this house its Regency flavour, for other influences are evident in the design. Some houses in Brant County, built before 1859, had a Greek porch similar to the one in PLATE 60, but flanked by treillage verandas, a curious arrangement sometimes found elsewhere. Most of these are gone: a surviving example in Oakland Township has a porch with arches and pilasters, classical rather than Greek, but it serves to illustrate the type.

These verandas had various functions besides reducing the 'boxiness' of plain rectangular houses. Their function as an outdoor sitting place was rather less important than it became later. They provided a dry and sheltered walk where ladies could take mild exercise without wading in mud or snow. They gave some protection to walls and foundations, but above all they shaded the rooms – the very thing for which they were eventually to be condemned. The newcomers from overseas seem to have been much more impressed by the heat of the Canadian summers than by the cold winters which, after all, they had been told to expect. They were inclined to build their houses to be cool and to ward off the glare of the frequent sunshine. The sun faded carpets and rotted hangings, and they had not yet learned its value as a source of heat in winter, or how to restrict heat and cold with shutters, slatted without and solid within. Though the idea of extensive verandas may have originated with retired officers who had served in the Indies, East or West, it soon became widely popular and remained so for about a century.

The examples in this collection that show the Regency influence most plainly happen to be built of stone and to be of the one-and-a-half storey type. The finest by far is the cobblestone farmhouse in PLATE 17. This is also, probably, the earliest. The proportions are so good that it comes as rather a shock to realize that the bold string course at the level of the upper window-sills probably indicates the former existence of a veranda on three sides which would mask the whole lower storey. This would most likely have been of treillage, and a somewhat later cobblestone house, not far from this one, has in fact such a veranda. These two houses built in the 1840s seem to be the earliest of a group of cobblestone buildings in Sidney Township, including the church in PLATE 65.

The little house beside Bethesda Church in Alnwick Township (PLATE 36) is perhaps more typically an 'Ontario farmhouse' than any other in this collection. A rather late example, it has a distinct Regency feeling and the French windows would seem to indicate that a veranda was intended. This may have been removed when the fieldstone walls were plastered. The stone house in PLATE 27 may also have lost a front veranda. It may be a little earlier than the Alnwick house, and could as easily have housed an 'honest English farmer' as the two-storeyed house described by John MacTaggart. The house in PLATE 38 not only has the steep roof still common in this eastern region, but shows increased height to the eaves which would make the attic almost a 'three-quarter storey', adding a good deal to the comfort of the upper rooms. A veranda would have reduced the look of height in this case.

Window glass in larger sizes was available before 1830, and windows with twelve larger panes and lighter bars began to replace the old many-paned types. In more remote and recent settlements, where breakage in transit might still be considerable, the smaller sizes were used well into the 1850s and they lingered nearly as long in some long-settled areas, whether from custom or as a minor economy. Long French windows, 'opening on the floor', as Alexander Hamilton of Queenston put it in 1833, began to be used before 1830, and have survived in a few instances from the following decade. They were used more frequently after 1840, and before long the hinged sashes began to be glazed in a special way, with good-sized panes on the inner side of each leaf and much narrower ones towards the jambs to form a kind of vertical border. This glazing is used in the Wolverton house (PLATE 31) in windows of ordinary length. It was also used for side-lights and transoms, the border being often carried across the top and bottom of the sash as well, and is found on the doors of china cupboards and bookcases.

The difference in feeling between a Loyalist Neo-classic house and houses showing strong Regency influence can be seen by comparing Poplar Hall with the Wolverton house and the house in PLATE 18, though the latter two show the mixture of influences already mentioned. The Wolverton house is influenced by the 'picturesque' to the extent of having a Gothic window in the gable. The house at Grafton (PLATE 18) has some resemblance to the older house standing immediately to the west, but the designer has used similar features in a way that produces a different effect. The Richardson house (PLATE 24) at first glance seems quite typical, but closer examination reveals some unusual features in addition to the plan without hall or lobby and with entrances directly into both parlour and living-room. The family date this house to the early forties, and this agrees quite well with the interior detail and with the use of a parlour stove to supplement two large open hearths, one above the other at the east (right-hand) end. The veranda has been cited above to illustrate the earlier type, but the method of suggesting flat arches simply with slender bars may belong to a later phase. That the curved parts spring well down the chamfered part of the posts could suggest that these bars have been inserted.

In the Upper Canadian countryside the Greek Revival normally involved little more than the use of Greek details instead of those taken from Roman work, whether the latter were derived directly or from the architecture of the Renaissance. Such details were usually applied to one or other of the forms of house already customary. Both five-bay and three-bay fronts might be treated in this way and the central doorway perhaps dignified by a porch the height of the main storey, with two columns, or four arranged in pairs, following pretty accurately one of the Greek orders and sometimes crowned with a fairly correct pediment. Often there was an attempt to give the block a temple-like outline by adjusting wall height and roof pitch and even carrying the main entablature right across the ends. To enhance the likeness to a temple, builders often adopted the type of house with its gable toward the road, which had already been favoured in villages and was sometimes found in the country. Such houses had normally three openings on each floor, the door at one side opening into a hall that might not run right through the house. Quite often there was a central chimney between two good-sized rooms on opposite sides of the house, but overlapping the chimneystack so that each might have a fireplace near a corner. The hall alongside the front room would be lengthened by the depth of the stack and the corresponding space beside the back room might be used for pantry, storeroom, or, perhaps, a little 'bed closet'. The arrangement upstairs might be similar, with two 'chambers' and such small bedrooms or bed closets as there might be space for. These houses did not give as much accommodation as the usual type with central entry and stairs, so they were frequently extended by wings on one or both sides. The type seems to have been favoured in Prince Edward County, where examples of various dates are fairly numerous. There are, however, a good many examples in other places, some with Greek details, while others follow other modes.

Another type of house becomes more common at this period (1835–45) and was to continue in fairly frequent use right through the century. This is a variant of the old rectangular house, but almost square in plan, with its roof hipped from all four sides to a short ridge or a flat. These houses usually have a central passage hall right through the house with the stairs towards the back. Their greater depth allowed all four rooms to be of fair size, even when two were larger than the others, and also allowed a longer straight run of stairs without making them too steep. When such houses have only one visible storey, and are perhaps surrounded by verandas, they have been placed in a special class and designated – not unreasonably – 'Regency cottages'. But two-storeyed houses of the type just described sometimes had the same enfolding verandas, often of treillage, though these have all too often disappeared. Others were given porches with columns, usually Greek in scale though not always showing a correct Greek order. Still others were given the full Greek treatment, with reasonably correct columns, antae, and entablatures, and a few even have full-scale columns rising from the main floor to an entablature below the eaves and supporting a large pediment.

Willowbank (PLATE 16) is a nearly square house of this type, and appears at first to be a full-fledged specimen of the Greek Revival. Closer examination reveals, however, that the details are mostly more Roman than Greek, and 'Classic Revival' seems a safer description. This house was planned in 1833. It has been attributed to an architect named Lathrop, 'from Tonawanda, New York', but, if Lathrop drew the first plan, he had little to do with building the house. Letters copied into Alexander Hamilton's letter book show that he sent to a 'Mr Latshaw', probably of Drummondville, U.C. (Niagara Falls, Ont.), a sketch of a house on a smaller scale than 'the former plan' and received from him a plan and 'elevation'. The first letter details a number of Hamilton's requirements, and further instructions are given in October, 1833, when he tells Latshaw that some of the stone has been 'hawled' to the site.

Some of Hamilton's instructions do not agree with the house as it stands. He wanted Tuscan columns 'fluted' instead of Ionic; possibly Latshaw pointed out the solecism. There were to be 'sheds' at either end of the west front (PLATE 16 shows the east façade) with a 'gallery' between them under which steps would lead up to the little porch at the 'hall door'. The existing curving steps therefore represent a change of plan or a later alteration. The same may be said of the French doors opening on to the east gallery and the three open hearths on the main floor. Hamilton had rejected 'windows opening on the floor', and had definitely said he would have only stoves and no fireplaces. Other letters show that Hamilton provided lumber and hardware as well as stone, but do not give the source of the other materials. The house was not yet finished in June 1835, and at the beginning of December he was inquiring about the Franklin stoves needed to heat it. However, he had moved in by February 15, 1836.

The Greek taste lasted into the 1850s, though unmixed examples become rarer in domestic work. Entrance porches decorated with Greek columns are found on houses that show little other trace of Greek influence. There are some houses in the Head of Lake Ontario area that have recessed porches like that of the Wolverton house (PLATE 31), but with two columns *in antis* in line with the outer wall. Houses with free-standing Greek porches are fairly common west of the Grand River and occasionally found elsewhere. The group in Brant County has already been mentioned but there are a number in Norfolk and Elgin Counties. The one shown in PLATE 60 is not entirely typical, for two-storeyed examples are usually square with hipped roofs. In this case the Doric porch is the only Greek feature unless we include the brick pilasters. These, it is true, derive from a feature sometimes used to give a church, hall, or even a house a closer resemblance to a temple. Pilasters, proportioned after Greek antae, would be carried across the end or all visible sides of a building, supporting a full entablature, to give a vaguely columnar effect without the use of expensive columns. Later such pilasters came to be used in vernacular building without any reference to a temple effect. Their capitals and bases were sometimes of wood, but often both caps and entablature were entirely of brick arranged ingeniously in bands of varying width, projection and pattern to suggest the various members of an order. In the house in PLATE 60 the pilasters support nothing and must once have been a decidedly disturbing factor. An old photograph shows them and the arches over the windows in 'white' brick, contrasting sharply with the red brick walls and making the front seem crowded and restless. Painting the whole in one tone of red has certainly improved the appearance of this house.

The other influence at work from the thirties on was the Romantic or Picturesque, represented at first in Upper Canada by the 'Gothic', an inclusive term which covered a good deal that derived more from Tudor work than from the mediaeval. It is possible that Gothic was first applied to churches, though only a few examples built before 1830 show any trace of it. Some houses built in the thirties show tentative attempts at Gothic, usually confined to gables or dormers inserted in the roof with windows in them of a faintly Gothic form. As often as not the house below these romantic gables had sash windows with twelve large panes and an ordinary Regency doorway – this lack of picturesqueness being slightly veiled by a veranda with a little Gothic detail. Interior details, such as mantels, might also be purely classical, as they were in Holland House, the first castellated house in Toronto.

In another instance, which can be firmly dated to 1834, a square frame house, of moderate size, has a hipped roof and Regency details except for the three front windows of the upper storey. These have pointed arches, although they are fitted with double-hung sashes. Small pointed lights in an enclosed porch, sheltering an entrance on the north side, may be later, but the bedroom windows seem to be original.* Another house, of dressed fieldstone, is raised on a high basement and has a straight-topped doorway and four large, twelve-pane windows shaded by a narrow veranda, all very Regency in feeling. Its low-pitched, ridged roof is, however, broken in front by three small gables, each with a little pointed window, the larger, end ones with two lights, a mullion and an attempt at tracery in the head. These windows have a slightly ecclesiastical air, and, in fact, the house is reported to have been inspired by 'an English abbey', but no resemblance to a conventual building has been achieved. In the case of 'Blythe', the dressed-timber house built by John Langton for his parents in 1836, not only was the T-shaped plan based on a late-mediaeval 'yeoman's' house, but the roofs had a steep pitch and the double-hung windows were given a Gothic air by coupling them in pairs separated by a mullion and indicating arches at the top of

* This house was built by the purchaser of the Dunbar Moodie farm in Hamilton Township near Port Hope, soon after the Moodies left in 1834, and was sold not long after to a Mr Holdsworth, whose descendants occupied it until quite recently. It has an unusual plan, has always been well cared for, has been little altered and is at present in good hands.

these lights. At 'The Beehive', built farther down Sturgeon Lake in 1839 for the Durnsford family with John Langton's aid and advice, the windows were coupled on a mullion in the same way, but here the sashes seem to have been long casements two panes wide and an H plan was used.*

All these examples were built by well-to-do colonists seeking a more picturesque form of 'cottage'. They would probably have been more numerous and decidedly more Gothic if Upper Canadian builders had been better versed in Gothic forms in the 1830s. By the mid-forties it was evidently easier to find craftsmen who could carry out more elaborate Gothic details, and certain books had been published containing designs that could, with some adjustment, be carried out in the materials available in Canada and did not, like the cottages in some earlier books, depend for picturesqueness on roofs of heavy thatch. The most influential of these publications was probably John Claudius Loudon's *An Encyclopaedia of Cottage, Farm, and Villa Architecture and Furniture* in the edition of 1833, for the American sources borrowed ideas and even actual designs from Loudon. The 'country houses' and 'cottage residences' in Andrew Jackson Downing's various works, published between 1841 and 1852, have designs that seem to owe a good deal to Loudon, but not to be actual copies. Whoever provided the editor of *Godey's Lady's Book* with specimens of 'model cottages' for a series begun in 1847, on the other hand, took most of them from Loudon, probably without leave asked or given.

A few houses in Ontario, built about 1848–55, seem to derive their inspiration from individual examples in Loudon's *Encyclopaedia*, possibly through the medium of Godey. In each case there has been considerable adjustment due to changes of materials and plan. In one case the builder was so determined to use a symmetrical front like one shown in both Loudon and Godey that he made a false 'front door' part of his central feature, against which a partition abuts on the inside. Three 'model cottages' published by Godey in the last months of 1847 are not taken from Loudon or Downing. All three seem to have influenced builders in Canada West, and the first and last represent trends which were to be widespread in that province and often to be combined in the same house. The first example, titled 'A Cottage in the old English style. By John Robertson, Esq., Architect', is a full-fledged specimen of a style also known as 'Cottage Gothic', 'Hudson Valley Gothic' and, in the 1890s, as 'Queen Anne'! The most noticeable features of this mode are the steep-pitched roofs, usually covering rather narrow wings, so that the gables are tall and sharply pointed. The edges of these gables are, in the first full phase of the style, decorated with stout wooden loops which writhe snake-like from a pinnacle at the peak to heavy drops at the lower angles of the eaves. These represent the cusped and traceried 'barge-boards' (verge boards) found on fifteenth and sixteenth century English houses. They seem to derive from the habit of artists who used a few curved strokes, much over-scaled, to delineate this tracery in their sketches – a convention used by the illustrators of Loudon's books. Looped barge-boards do not seem to be very common in England; possibly, with actual examples before them, English builders understood

* These statements are based on measured drawings made a good many years ago for Dr Eric Arthur, when he was about to publish his first small brochure on early Ontario buildings. These drawings are now in the Ontario Archives.

this shorthand. American builders, however, seem to have been more literal.

Cottage Gothic thus could derive from Loudon and Downing, but typical examples have a character that differentiates them from the designs found in those sources. This may be due to greater height, especially noticeable in the gable ends. Built as a rule in sections one-room wide, arranged on a +, T, or H plan, they are usually under two storeys, but steep roofs and higher walls combine to give excellent head room on the upper floor. At the sides the greater height of wall is masked by overhanging eaves and sometimes verandas. It is revealed in the ends, and these tall, fretted gables with the lesser gables, sharply pointed or hooded, that serve as dormers give these houses their picturesque outlines and, when skilfully handled, their charm.

These early specimens of Cottage Gothic, like the other Gothic houses of 1845–55, are more often found in or near the towns, but the style was quickly seized upon by rural builders as a means of giving a conventional house a fashionable air. That fashion rather than picturesqueness was usually the object is shown by the way houses of quite ordinary shape and plan were dressed up with a little 'Gothic' detail, without any attempt to vary the outline or giving the roof a steep pitch. The pitch of the roof was important, for the centre-hall house, nearly square on plan, with a rear wing or 'ell', could be given a satisfactory appearance from the side if the gables were steep enough. The effect could be enhanced by giving a summer kitchen or woodshed, at the end of the ell, a cross-gable large enough to balance the main one, suggesting an H plan. However, with the greater depth now common, a roof of moderate pitch would give an adequate half storey, and where such broad, low gables were retained and decorated with looped and scrolled barge boards, the effect is far from pleasing. Some builders abandoned the centre hall and used a T-shaped plan, with the entrance and stairs placed near the junction of the two wings. Such houses are turned so that the cross-wing presents a gable to the road, while the dining-room and kitchen across the hall in the longer wing get more sunlight and a better view.

The examples of gabled buildings with barge-boards in this collection are all rather late and not entirely typical. The house in Foxboro (PLATE 48) illustrates the later method of making barge-boards with fretsawed scrolls instead of built up loops and cusps. The same method is used in more skimpy fashion on the Sophiasburgh Township Hall (PLATE 59). Neither building is consistently Gothic and both are tending to mid-Victorian fantasy. The house in Scarborough Township (PLATE 71) shows a scheme resorted to when it was felt that a decorated peak did not give enough interest to a narrow front. By projecting a two-storied porch, sometimes flanked by verandas, a little 'movement' was produced, but in frame buildings these narrow porches tend to increase the look of excessive height which was beginning to characterize many of the smaller houses of the time. The fruit barn in PLATE 55 illustrates very well the way this style was applied to stables, coach-houses, and woodsheds (rarely to barns). For contrast with an older manner, it may be compared to the waggon shop in PLATE 57.

The last two buildings cited show a form of wall-covering which became generally popular at about the same time that Cottage Gothic was making its appearance, and which was often combined with it. Vertical siding had, of course, been used much earlier. The French Canadians seem to have used it from the seventeenth century to protect walls with frames filled with dressed timber or some other material. Since the walls were filled it was not essential to use battens to cover the cracks. Settlers of German origin in Markham Township and adjoining areas seem to have begun quite early to cover walls with vertical siding, using rather narrow boards, apparently with rabbets or tongue-and-groove joints. Later these boards become still narrower and the joints are sometimes beaded like interior wainscot. Battens are more rarely found in these areas than elsewhere.

'Board and batten' makes its appearance about 1850. Downing in the 1844 edition of his *Cottage Residences* has 'a villa in the Italian style, bracketed', the walls certainly covered with vertical siding and probably with board and batten. In December 1847, Godey published plans and perspective of a farmhouse, reprinted from the *Albany Cultivator* to which they had been sent by 'J. E. Scott, Toledo, Ohio'. These show a simple frame farmhouse, not unlike some built in Canada in the late 1850s, but in the 'bracketed' style and pretty certainly intended to be covered with board and batten. In its simplest form this type of covering consists of boards of moderate width, left rough and nailed vertically to the frame as close together as possible, with narrow strips or battens (up to three inches in width) nailed over the cracks. When neatness was desired, the boards and battens might be dressed on the outside to take paint better, the battens moulded and even finished at the top with attractive little arches, as in the school in PLATE 67. More often the upper ends of the battens are hidden by a strip, plain or moulded, directly under the eaves, as in the lodge in PLATE 73 or the church in PLATE 70. Vertical siding was sometimes applied to dressed-log houses and has been stripped off to show the timbers. In at least some cases it appears not to have been sufficiently air-tight; the battens were removed towards the end of the century and the boards covered with tongue-and-groove cove siding. In one such case there was a layer of horizontal boarding on the inside of the frame under the lath and plaster, so the house has now four 'skins' and is certainly easy to heat.

The covering of frame or log houses with roughcast or with smooth plaster became more common in the 1830s and lasted through the century. Plaster was believed to be a warmer covering than wood and, for the reasons already touched on, there may have been something in this idea. Roughcast appealed to Scots accustomed to 'harled' stonework, and it was felt to 'go' with Gothic. Many people evidently preferred the neat finish of smooth plaster to any form of boarding and even to rough stonework. The house in PLATE 66 shows the effect of smooth plaster, in this case possibly on masonry of some kind. Brick houses were occasionally plastered as a protection against damp. It is not uncommon to find an east gable treated in this way. One house in Markham Township had the upper part of its east wall covered with vertical siding with grooved joints, showing the lines of the roofs of a destroyed shed and veranda. There are, however, instances of brick fronts thinly plastered, painted red or buff and marked with lines to indicate a superior even-coloured brick without the delightful variations of the common brick at the sides. As a rule brickwork was considered neat and elegant enough, more so, it would seem, than all but the most careful stonework. In areas where stone was plentiful, after brick became readily obtainable, we find buildings with random rubble back and end walls, and with neat fronts of red brick!

Our ancestors' attitude to stonework was very different from ours. Smooth-dressed ashlar in good-sized blocks and laid in regular courses was, as it has always been, the most magnificent material possible. Rockfaced blocks were permissible for rustication in appropriate places and in appropriately large scale. Rubble, carefully dressed, sized and coursed might make a respectable front, but, to attain elegance, it was better to plaster it, paint the plaster stone colour, and mark it out in blocks of proper size. Of course, no one who came within a hundred feet of the building was fooled by these subterfuges, but the desired effect was obtained at slight expense and besides it made the house warmer. This pursuit of neatness and elegance led to still more curious practices. The walls of frame houses were often covered with flush boarding, dressed smooth and lined or grooved in blocks. The walls were painted blue-grey, light grey, or pale buff; the lines touched with white and the whole sometimes sanded. Raised quoins are sometimes indicated at the corners, and in a few cases the 'joints' are grooved deeply enough to suggest a light rustication over the whole wall. The church at Vittoria (PLATE 28) was given a fairly full treatment of this kind, though the lining of the walls is a good deal obscured by later painting. It is hard to believe that anyone was expected to take these innocent deceptions seriously, even in the eighteenth century. When handled with a good sense of proportion, the effect is often good and the bolder scale is a relief from the busy surfaces produced by clapboard or vertical siding. A later form, in which the 'blocks' were outlined by half-round strips more than an inch wide, painted white on a blue-grey, can hardly have been intended to deceive even at a distance. Nevertheless, this 'dishonesty' offended the moral sense of the later Victorians, strengthened by the tenets of Ruskin and Morris, and examples of such treatment are becoming steadily rarer, although generations given to the use of more naturalistic and uglier forms of imitation stone, brick, clapboard, and shingles can hardly condemn them on grounds of falsity.

The 'Italian' or 'Bracketed' style, mentioned in connection with vertical siding, was another phase of the Picturesque being publicized in the late 1830s and 1840s. It had made its appearance before 1845, but its full impact came after 1850. There were two phases – the first deriving from the early work of John Nash based on a type of north-Italian farmhouse or 'villa-farm' and characterized by broad eaves and, very often, a squat tower with a low-pitched hipped roof. In one well-known example the eaves are decorated with the little scallops cut from solid board as used by Nash in his 'Swiss' style. The other type is of Tuscan inspiration; it has bracketed eaves, round-arched windows often grouped in pairs, and towers of taller and more slender proportions. The Italian is on the whole a town style, though it is sometimes found in small villages or in the country. The style made some contributions to the vernacular building of 1845–65, in particular bracketed cornices and projecting eaves, with or without brackets. The inn at Cashel (PLATE 26) shows bracketed eaves applied to a building without other Italianate features. The earlier brackets are of the type used here, based on classic console, projecting horizontally as much as two or three feet with little vertical depth. Later they became more vertical and the resemblance to a console becomes steadily vaguer until in the last quarter of the century eaves brackets assume fantastic shapes (PLATES 74, 77, and 85). In some cases they are reminiscent of measuring worms which have humped their way up the wall until stopped by the projecting eaves. Another legacy of the villa may be the habit of grouping windows in pairs separated by a heavy mullion or a pier. This arrangement, common from the late 1860s on, is a good deal less satisfactory, visually and functionally, than the three-light window which it tends to replace.

It has already been pointed out that the middle decades of the nineteenth century saw a great deal of building in most of the southern part of Ontario. It was during these years that there evolved a vernacular architecture which was spread across the province, showing just enough regional differences to make these variations an interesting study. To some extent this was a synthesis of the various imported fashions outlined above, and resemblances can therefore be traced to buildings in various parts of the United States, in Britain or even, occasionally, in Quebec. Nevertheless, these buildings have in general a characteristic and recognizable 'Upper Canadian' flavour, more discernible perhaps to observant visitors from outside the province than to the inhabitants. A good many of the buildings illustrated are examples of this vernacular style, hardly to be classified under any one of the styles described. Among the most satisfying is the fieldstone house in PLATE 30, but PLATES 26, 54, and 66 may also be cited.

This was very much a builder's style, seldom owing anything directly to a professed architect, even if we apply the term in the elastic meaning of the time. Details might be derived from books published by architects, but the design was worked out by the builder, whether carpenter, bricklayer, or mason, under the instructions of his client. These last might be almost excessively detailed, including sketch plans or even elevations, or they might consist simply of directions to build a house 'like So-and-so's', with a smaller parlour, an extra fireplace, a better woodshed, or some other change. The success of the design would in any case depend on the craftsman's skill and the almost intuitive feeling for proportion and scale derived from a sound training in his craft. It is rightness of proportions that makes most of these buildings so satisfying, sometimes in spite of the details derived from pattern books. Attempts at fine architecture are exceptional and not always successful, but even the most modest buildings seldom fall below the prevailing high standard of design and construction.

Until after 1840 the preparation of materials for building was largely carried out by hand. Planks, boards, and sometimes framing timbers came from the sawmill, which might also produce sawn blocks and slabs from which shingles and laths might be riven. Such details as sash, doors, shutters, trim inside and out, and mantelpieces were made on the spot by the carpenter or the joiner, who ran his own mouldings and even did turning when required. In the 1830s planing mills had been established in the United States and were turning out Greek detail by waterpowered machines. How much of their product found its way to Upper Canada is not certain. There is evidence that fine mantelpieces were brought across the lake from Rochester for a house in Port Hope, finished in 1834, and others of the kind have been found in Cobourg. It seems not unlikely that other details used for this house may have come from the same source, but the inside trim varies slightly from room to room which suggests that it was turned out on the job, or at least made to order at the Rochester mill. This trim is a larger version of the type used externally on the old inn at Normandale (PLATE 19). In this case the square plaques at the upper corners mostly contain leaf designs, apparently carved in wood. Two other houses in the vicinity had lion masks in the corners, moulded in plaster but painted like the wood. Occasionally the squares were plain, but usually they contained a turned roundel. Such details lent themselves to mass-production, and it is possible that some sawmill owners had installed planing machinery before 1840, and even more likely that there were already chair factories and turneries with water-powered lathes. Turneries certainly existed by the later forties, and a few specialized planing mills are listed in 1851 which had probably been started some years before.

The use of prepared woodwork naturally brought some standardization. This can be observed in the recurrence of certain mouldings which give some indication of date, though some mills went on using the same knives for a long time. Houses built after 1865 sometimes have the same inside trim as was used ten or twelve years earlier, regardless of the change in fashion. At first there was a good deal of individuality in the application of these stock details, and some mills provided a fairly wide selection of mouldings and other details and would do special custom work. Once a knife had been ground for a special order, however, there was usually nothing to prevent its being used again and again. It is quite possible that, when the same pilastered doorway appears on several houses in a village or a neighbourhood, the stock-in-trade of a particular mill is responsible rather than the examples in the local builder's pattern book. Many more turneries and planing mills are listed in 1857. The latter are often combined with 'sash and door factories' (later 'sash, door & blind') and powered by steam. By this time the newly completed railways were making the products of these mills available over wider areas. Partly because of the lessening use of handicrafts and the increasing standardization, some people would choose 1855 as a terminal date for the early building of the province. In fact the mid-fifties did see the end of one epoch and the beginning of a new one, but such dates cannot be rigidly applied. The change, in this respect, came slowly and unevenly; a sharp dividing line drawn at 1855, or even 1867, would exclude much that belongs with the older time, for instance the two little stone churches in PLATES 46 and 49.

With the late 1850s and the 1860s we are entering the period of high Victorian fantasy with all its bizarre eclecticism, its tendency to display, to intricacy, and to over-elaboration of detail. In furniture and bric-a-brac these tendencies followed soon after the Great Exhibition held in the Crystal Palace in London, England, in 1851. Fortunately it took a few years before architecture in Canada was much affected, and still longer before the new mode reached the country builder. In the towns some buildings erected close to 1860 look like adaptations of the Italian mode, but already show some suggestion of French Second Empire taste and some features of the style that became common after 1865. Their walls are often treated with large, slightly recessed panels, surrounded by plain bands of brickwork. Windows often have the curved heads, arched on the segment of a circle, characteristic of the sixties and seventies, or are round-arched. They are usually rather narrow and high, so that when, as is often the case, the old type of sash with three panes to a row is used, more rows are needed than the normal four. Glass was now available in large sizes, and arrangements of larger panes, like the eight-pane windows in the Township Hall at Grafton (PLATE 50), are sometimes found. The Sophiasburgh Township Hall (PLATE 59) shows the tall narrow windows and a consistent use of the segmental arch combined with 'Gothic' detail, but the wall panels here are not the kind just referred to, but derive from an earlier type. In several of these buildings the windows are decorated with cast-iron archivolts, pediments, or entablatures supported by brackets, and these iron ornaments, representing stone, were themselves occasionally reproduced in wood.

The few country examples of this new mode are later in date than those in the towns. It is notable that the examples of houses published in George Brown's *Canada Farmer* in 1864 are all Cottage Gothic except for a round-log house, and even this has a pinnacle at the apex of its peak. These plans and elevations were made by James Smith, a Toronto architect, who in 1865 provided plans, elevation, and section for a good-sized, square house of two storeys, much more in the current style. In this case all the openings in the five-bay front have segmental heads, decorated with rather massive, plain archivolts with raised keystones and 'formed out of stone, fine tooled'. The centre bay is projected eighteen inches (the thickness of the walls) in both storeys and is crowned by a pediment-like gable above the eaves cornice. The eaves project about three feet, supported by heavy brackets, and break out around the central projection. The windows are tall for their width and there is, altogether, a greater emphasis on height. The design is not Italianate, but evidently derives from the version of 'Louis XIV' favoured in France at this time.

A good many houses which can be dated just before 1867 show features derived from this style, though few of them depart so far as this from the vernacular manner. They are usually two-storeyed and of some size, often with verandas on three sides, supported by stout square posts with chamfers starting rather high and with some form of fretsawed arching or bracketing. This fretsaw work is somewhat restrained, for the more elaborate and fantastic patterns are later in date. By 1867 the 'Second Empire' influence becomes more marked and begins to relate more definitely to the 'mansard roof' style, which began to take hold in the cities at that time, and through the seventies and eighties remained an alternative to the gabled and other styles, especially with the speculative builder. Few houses in the country have mansard roofs, for their owners did not often require an attic that was practically a full third floor. There were, however, a few examples, complete even to a little tower over the porch with its own small mansard and, perhaps, flanked by bay windows.* Besides these larger examples there are some houses with one storey and a mansard. These are smaller in area and often quite attractive, though the smallest ones tend to be reminiscent of an old-fashioned game pie with a raised crust. Much more numerous are the houses with roofs hipped to a ridge, a flat, or a glazed belvedere – with three-bay fronts sometimes shorter than the sides and with either long sash windows opening on verandas or one or two bay windows.

The details of the mansard style eventually lose the traces of its French origin and become dissolved in the complication of late-Victorian woodwork. The store at Lakefield (PLATE 74) is a late example and illustrates this tendency. It has the mansard roof, the characteristic round-arched dormer windows and segmental window heads in the middle storey, but the ornament of the dormers, involving turned elements, suggests that it may be as late as 1890. The windows also have their sashes divided by a single vertical glazing bar, giving four large panes to a window. This type of glazing came in soon after 1860; all the houses published in the *Canada Farmer* in 1864–69 show this kind of sash in all the larger windows, but it was some years before it became the rule. In the seventies this was the standard form, varied occasionally by the eight-pane window already mentioned. A late example of this pattern of glazing appears in the larger windows of the school in PLATE 77, which may be a little earlier than the store at Lakefield. This school, unusually large for one in the country, shows the gable style in its later development. The small gable has the characteristic unstructural tie-beam and kingpost, almost lost in the elaboration of pierced barge-boards. The little porches show the curve or 'kick' in the roof not uncommon in the 1880s, and the slender, chamfered posts which returned to use at that time. Usually there would be fretsaw brackets at the top of such posts or a band of spindles between them.

The large house at Blackstock in PLATE 88 may be described as a version of the 'Tuscan villa' in the style of the seventies and early eighties. The block plan and general outline recall the Italianate villas of some twenty years before, but no single detail is Italian. With mansards substituted for the pitched roofs, this house would be a very full expression of the mansard style. It is remarkably well preserved and does not seem to have lost any of its vulnerable wooden ornament. This is a *good* example of the work of its period, which cannot be said of many such ambitious efforts of contemporary designers. These are often no more than ill-assorted conjunctions of ugly details, possessing at best a kind of horrible fascination. In this case the designer has managed to produce an effect of unity and dignity, in spite of the style in which he was working.

The bay-windowed house in PLATE 85 is also a specimen of the Late Victorian at its

* Such towers and bay windows with some other details formed, of course, no part of the style of Louis XIV, but they are included in the version found in French domestic architecture in the later nineteenth century.

height and by no means a bad one. The black-and-white print does not convey the full impact of the building, for the designer has made as much play with variations of colour as with form and texture. Apart from the contrast of the red brick walls with the pale buff of the 'white' brick trim, the bluish slate roof is patterned in light grey and a rosy red, while the darker grey of the cast-stone keystones, with moulded Scotch thistles, seems to punctuate the whole composition. On the whole the various elements have been handled with a good deal of skill and, below the eaves, with some restraint, though the flat-roofed porch, which evidently once existed between the bays, may have struck a note of greater intricacy.

The verandas of the Blackstock house show one of the forms found in the 1880s, with elaborate fretsaw brackets extending from the tops of the slender posts. Another form which originated in this decade and continued into the 1890s is illustrated by the little porch of the post office at Bethany (PLATE 86). This form has a band of turned spindles extending from one post to the next, the motive being often echoed in a balustrade, if there is one, or perhaps in the decoration of a gable. Verandas like these are often found on much older houses, either as a replacement or an addition. Either there was a high mortality of early stoops after 1870, or a 'modern' veranda was felt to be an easy way of smartening up a shabby old dwelling. Now these verandas are, in many cases, going the way of those they replaced. Unfortunately there was another easy way of modernization by removing old sashes and replacing them with the large-paned variety currently in style. Again and again an early house is found practically unchanged except that all conspicuous windows have been resashed. This process has been half-heartedly carried out in the case of the store at Cashel (PLATE 26), where the two types of sash present a contrast which would be more marked if the frames and sashes were painted a light tone. There is the same contrast between the resashed windows of the white house to the left in PLATE 43 and the darker-walled house on the right which has retained its old sash. The little stone house near Williamsburg (PLATE 23) shows how much the harmony of scale and proportion can be upset in a plain front by the loss of sash bars, but this can perhaps best be assessed by considering how much the house in PLATE 30 would lose if its lower windows had been treated like the ones in the house at Kirk Hill (PLATE 54).

While the larger and sophisticated works of the country builder, whether with direct assistance from an architect or not, were following more or less closely the city fashions, the simpler vernacular manner of building was running to seed. The sure sense of proportion was weakening, and the ordinary, unpretentious Ontario farmhouse was becoming less and less an attractive cottage, blending satisfactorily with its surroundings, and tending more and more to be a tall, gaunt box, pierced symmetrically with blank, uninteresting windows and dull doorways. The change had begun in the sixties, but was then often modified by verandas and, in some brick houses, by bands of patterned brick-work inserted under the eaves apparently in an attempt to lessen the look of excessive height. This latter expedient was not possible in frame buildings, and it is in the frame houses that this increasing grimness begins to be really noticeable as the seventies advance. A slight trace of it may even be discerned in the stone house in PLATE 90. This, however, is a pleasing example where ornamental details have been used, not unskilfully, to give a touch of picturesqueness.

It is hardly necessary to follow the course of rural building on into the early years of this century. It was hardly affected at all by the various Late Victorian movements which brought some change in the cities and are held to have opened the way for later developments. On the whole rural building in Ontario grew progressively duller from the late 1890s, with a tendency to eschew all fantasy without producing anything better.

So far the remarks have dealt chiefly with domestic buildings, which, after all, make up the majority. Of the other types, inns, stores, schools, and halls follow the same styles as the houses and have sometimes been cited as examples of them. Churches, however, follow a rather different, though related, development. The first churches were practically all of the 'meeting-house' type and mostly conceived in a simple version of the Neo-classic style. The body of the church had, normally, a rectangular 'temple' form, though there are one or two square examples. Anglicans, Scottish Presbyterians, and Roman Catholics usually added a small tower at one end, often supporting an open belfry with a short spire above. Apses and chancels were rare, though the first stone church in the province, at St. Andrews West, has an apse the full width of the church. By the 1820s it was beginning to be felt that Gothic was the proper style for churches, and the result was a curious mixed style with a good deal of charm, resembling the Gothic of England in the eighteenth century. The tall triple-hung sash windows, differing only in their height from those in the houses, were now given pointed arches and the glazing bars of their highest sashes were made to interlace so as to form a simple type of tracery. In some cases these windows are the only suggestion of Gothic in the whole building; for doorway, tower, belfry, and spire the builder goes back to the Neo-classic details with which he was familiar. The United Church at Kirk Hill (PLATE 32), though it dates from the 1840s, illustrates this mixture of styles very well. The graceful tower and spire are of a type known from drawings to have existed on several churches built between 1815 and 1830 (and one or two earlier ones),though most of these have disappeared, either destroyed with the church or replaced with something Gothic. At the entrance is a good-sized portico, also classic in design. If the rather broad windows ever had the kind of sash just described, they have given place to mullions and transoms, with quatrefoils pierced between the pointed heads of the long lights in the manner of what is called 'plate tracery'. Simple tracery of this kind was often inserted in the windows of early churches when they were being made more Gothic to conform to later fashions.

The church at Grafton (PLATE 20) is fairly close in date to the one at Kirk Hill, but presents a sharp contrast. It is much more consistently Gothic, but the builder seems to have been inspired by certain stone churches built in Scotland after the Reformation and representing a partial survival of late Gothic forms. The tower especially is like some Scottish towers of the sixteenth and seventeenth centuries. There is a rather similar stone church tower near Grenville on the Quebec bank of the Ottawa, but I know of no other in Ontario. The attempt to translate stone forms into wood has not been entirely successful and perhaps this church should be described as quaint. In the church at Hazzard (PLATE 61), the proportions are, for some reason, particularly satisfying. Here Gothic features are confined to upper windows and the simple little pinnacles at the corners of the belfry. The whole effect seems reminiscent of New England, though it is hard to say just why this is so.

These churches, with those in PLATES 42 and 65, show a marked time lag, for by the early forties churches in the towns and some in the country were being designed in a manner much closer to the more developed Gothic Revival used in England in 1800–30. Though this Gothic was still handled in a much freer way than the correct and scholarly Gothic that followed it, it had been purged of classical detail. St. John's, Jordan (PLATE 14), shows this tendency at work and also the tendency to favour the later period of English mediaeval architecture whose 'perpendicular' tracery was comparatively easy to render in wood. Perhaps the most extreme case of time lag is the United Church at North Gower (PLATE 68). Nothing about this building except the inscribed date would suggest that it was built in 1870, and it is strange to think that this church, little Trinity the Marsh (PLATE 70), and St. John's Lutheran (PLATE 49) were probably all built in the same decade.

Not all churches of this period were Gothic; simple vernacular meeting-houses were built in the 1850s, and some more ambitious churches used a classic style. Like a few examples in the earlier period, these might have round-arched openings, and in some churches of the forties it is hard to say whether the designer intended a Roman style or a simplified Romanesque. Christ Church, Vittoria, is definitely Renaissance, though whether the source of inspiration was English or Italian is not so clear. St. Anthony's (PLATE 46) and St. John's Lutheran seem again to hark back to an earlier time. It seems probable that the same builder was responsible for both these churches and for another little Lutheran church, between Waterloo and St. Agatha, which has points of resemblance to both but especially to St. Anthony's. The use of too rigid a terminal date for 'Early Ontario' buildings would exclude all three of these churches, one built in 1863, one in 1868 or 1869, and the third, St. John's, in 1873. The church at South Bay (PLATE 53) and Bethesda Church, Alnwick Township (PLATE 36) are later than the rest. Bethesda Church is plain vernacular Gothic, hardly typical of its period, though such simple churches are found as late as 1890. The round-arched openings in the South Bay church are not intended to be classic, but follow the contemporary fashion for Romanesque, in this case with a suggestion of North Italian origin. The wheel window looks quite Lombard. There are some other churches of the eighties where this influence is present in about the same degree. In this case also the complete absence of 'frills' is not entirely normal, for churches in this style are often loaded with elaborate brickwork in contrasting colour.

The purpose of this brief survey has been to give to those unfamiliar with the subject rather more information than could be included in the captions. Much has had to be left unsaid: planning, construction, and interior details are not illustrated and so could not be satisfactorily dealt with. Our main purpose has been to record some things that we have long enjoyed, and, in recording them, perhaps to share them.

Photographs

1 *Warsaw, Peterborough County*

This view of the northern outskirts of Warsaw, across the mill pond, seems to sum up the aspect of the Ontario countryside which these photographs are intended to record. It illustrates the quiet charm of places settled for more than a century. Dummer Township was opened for settlement about 1831, and the first mills at Warsaw were built within three or four years. The farmstead on the hill will have seen three or four generations, and the little church is not much younger.

1

2 *Dressed-log house, Glenelg Township, Grey County*

This, and the pictures that follow, represent the type of building which prevailed in each section of the province as it was opened up and for a generation or two after, though the proportion of log and timber buildings grew steadily less. The ordinary inhabitant of Upper Canada in the nineteenth century did not admire log buildings and welcomed their passing as a sign of progress. They were quite ready, as in this case, to conceal the timbers with a protective covering, as much to improve appearance as for an added defence against weather. The absence of open hearths and extra height of wall indicate a comparatively late date for this sturdy dressed-log house, and this agrees well enough with the date of settlement in this area.

3 *The Smith-Dalziel barn, Vaughan Township, York County*

Surviving examples of timber building vary greatly in date; this barn is among the oldest. It was built by John Smith (Schmidt) who bought the property in 1808 and soon built his great barn to house the stock brought from Pennsylvania. Sold to the Dalziels in 1829, Smith's barn and house now form part of the Black Creek Conservation Area. Restoration as a museum necessitated some changes – windows in the overhang, chinking of the upper part of the timber walls, and the glazing of a 'clean-out' hole. The framed overhang was intended from the first, but the 'outshots' to the north seem to be early additions. 'Bank' barns, with stables below, and 'overhangs' are 'Pennsylvania Dutch' features, but were adopted by settlers of other origins in Upper Canada. The bellcote visible beyond is on the woodshed of the brick house built by the Dalziels in the 1870s.

4 *Dressed-log house, Goulbourn Township, Carleton County*

This moderate-sized house, standing close beside the road, is more typical of the homes of the early settlers than the others photographed. It is situated in a region where log buildings are still quite numerous, and, as usual, difficult to date. In this area a date around 1830 would be quite possible, but the house may be a good deal later. During a long period of occupancy it seems to have undergone various alterations culminating in the modern roofing. The steep pitch of the roof is a regional feature. The house is now used as a storehouse.

5 *Dressed-log farm buildings, Goulbourn Township, Carleton County*

These buildings stand behind and to the right of the house in the previous plate. The relatively modern home of the present owner lies to the right of the laneway, and to the left is a third small and early dwelling. The farm buildings were obviously built piecemeal and are difficult to date. They are, however, typical of the small stables, etc., built by the settlers before, or as adjuncts to, storage barns. In this case no barn is in evidence.

6 *Poplar Hall, on Highway 2, Augusta Township, Grenville County*

An outstanding example of 'Loyalist Neo-classic' built about 1810–11 by William Wells east of the site of Maitland. The early date has been questioned, but is confirmed by the assessment rolls of the township. The county history is probably right in saying that it was in this house that Wells was captured by United States troops during the War of 1812, though the bullet holes supposed to have been once visible in the ceiling of one parlour may be more doubtful. The house has recently been restored, perhaps with too great enthusiasm, especially as regards the chimney stacks. The quaint four-column porch which was removed in this restoration may well have been original.

7 *The McFarland house, River Road, south of Niagara-on-the-Lake, Lincoln County*

This house was built by James McFarland in 1800. Older and simpler than Poplar Hall, it is perhaps a more typical example of the period before 1812. The narrow doorway, with its transom but no side-lights, is more common at this early date than it was later. Like the nearly contemporary DePuisaye House, the McFarland House was used as a military hospital during the War of 1812–15. The house is now the property of the Niagara Parks Commission and has been restored.

7

8 *The McCracken cabin, south of McCracken's Landing, Peterborough County*

This picturesque log dwelling was evidently built in sections. The higher central portion is of round logs and probably represents the original house dating from the settlement of Dummer Township in the early 1830s. The left-hand or north lean-to is of logs dressed on two sides, and is obviously an early addition; its massive chimney of local limestone rubble implies a large kitchen fireplace. The south lean-to is probably later and may be framed. There are further outshots at the other end, making that view even more irregular than this one.

9 *Frame house, on Highway 28, South Monaghan Township, Northumberland County*

Francis Page was granted the property on which this house stands and in 1823 had a small tavern on the road to Scott's Mills (later Peterborough). It is just possible that this building was used for the same purpose, for an early sketch of nearby Bailieboro shows two very similar houses, one of them certainly a tavern. The house probably dates from about 1830 and is of a type characteristic of the early period – one described in 1829 as typically 'Loyalist' or 'Yankee'.

10 *Temple of the Children of Peace (Willsonites), Sharon, York County*

This striking building, begun in 1825, possibly derives from the square churches or meeting-houses which the founder of the sect, David Willson, may easily have seen, as they were not uncommon in the old colonies. The square form and most of the details, however, have an esoteric symbolical significance. The curious construction with short clapboards between visible uprights is sometimes found in Norway and Sweden. Willson, born in Dutchess County, New York, in 1778, became a Quaker after coming to Upper Canada. He broke with one of the Yonge Street meetings, chiefly because of the prohibition of music in services. The sect he founded emphasized the duty of praise as well as prayer. They formed a co-operative agricultural community, and made missionary expeditions into neighbouring townships with a white-robed choir transported in a wagon. The sect continued into the 1860s and then gradually passed out of existence. The attraction of the building depends to a great extent on the excellence of its proportions. It is difficult to say how far these are due to the 'Prophet' or how far to Ebenezer Doan, the carpenter-builder.

11 *The shore of Lake Ontario looking west towards Newcastle harbour*

The harbour at the mouth of Wilmot Creek, now largely ruinous, was formed by a company about 1838 to serve their new village of 'Bond Head'. The village did not flourish, however, owing largely to the unhealthiness of its site and the fact that the early 1840s were bad years for 'fever and ague', almost certainly malaria. Nevertheless some houses remain from this period, and it was here that Daniel Massey had his first foundry, moved later to Newcastle – the village on Dundas Street (now Highway 2). Bond Head has been for many years part of the incorporated village of Newcastle. The point in the remote distance is Raby Head.

12 *The Haight-Zavitz house, near Sparta, Elgin County*

The older part of this house, between the large chimney-stack and the smaller chimney on the left, was built about 1820. Sparta is the centre of a Quaker settlement near the shores of Lake Erie; the Haight family were Quakers from Pennsylvania. The two entrance doors are a feature often found in houses built by settlers of German origin and regularly used by the stricter Mennonites. It is not known that this custom had any religious significance among the Quakers. The part to the right of the large chimney was added by the present owners in a style harmonizing with the old house.

13 *Churchville cemetery, Peel County*

Some of the many and interesting gravestones in this cemetery. The discoloured marker to the right is a wooden slab celebrating the memory of Amaziah Church, who built the first mills at Churchville about 1818, carrying the 'irons' from the lakeshore through the forest. This cemetery, besides being beautifully situated and well kept, is particularly rich in stones with unusual emblems and inscriptions, among them one, unfortunately broken, to Henry Moffat, an Irishman who died in 1867. The stone is decorated with various symbols of the Loyal Orange Order, including King William III on his white horse, and inscribed with the following verse:

'My glass soon run my grave you see
Prepare in time to follow me
Go home dear friends and shed no tears
I do lie here till Christ appears'.

Sacred
Memory
In Memory of
WHO DIED

14 *St. John's Anglican Church, Jordan, Lincoln County*

St. John's Church 'at the Twenty' was built in 1841. It shows, particularly in the windows, a somewhat more advanced and ambitious form of Gothic than was usual at that period. However, the designer had to use wood for his battlements, window tracery, and hood moulds, where a mediaeval architect would almost certainly have used stone. He has shown some degree of skill in adapting these to his material, but has used an almost classic form for his main gable.

15 *The Davey house, Bath, Lennox & Addington County*

The Davey family were among the early Loyalist settlers in Fredericksburg Township, and much of the village of Bath is built on their property. Their first house was on the lakeshore, and this house on the hill to the north may be their third. Built before 1820, it is a full example of the Loyalist Neo-classic. The interior details are outstanding, notably the mantlepiece in the drawing-room in the left-hand wing. The transom and side-lights of the doorway are similar to those on a stone building rather later in date belonging to this family, and may be later than the pilasters framing them. The half storey was lighted from the north side by dormer windows which were carefully kept off the front or south side. When the photograph was taken, only the drawing-room was being used in the old part of the house which was in some danger of destruction.

16 *Willowbank, near Queenston, Lincoln County*

Alexander Hamilton began to build Willowbank in 1833 and moved into the house before 14 February 1836, but not very long before. The house belongs to a small group of Ontario houses with pillared porticoes running the height of two storeys. In this case this arrangement and the extension of the portico across the whole of the east front may have been suggested by the house of Robert Hamilton, Alexander's father, at Queenston. However, Alexander omitted the upper gallery and substituted a small balcony over the door. The high basement, a full storey, contained the kitchen and service rooms.

17 *Cobblestone farmhouse, Sidney Township, Hastings County*

The earliest of the cobblestone buildings in Sidney Township has features characteristic of the early 1840s and yet is a fully developed example of the Regency style. It seems almost certain that it once was surrounded by treillage verandas, though it may well be felt that these would damage the subtle proportions of the building. Though very simple, the design is more sophisticated than the other stone examples of Regency illustrated in this collection. A cobblestone woodshed and summer kitchen project from the other end of the house at right angles to the small wing visible to the right of this photograph. It was from such finely proportioned buildings that the vernacular style at its best was developed.

18 *Brimley House, Grafton, Northumberland County*

This house was built by the owner of an older brick house, which stands a little to the right, for his daughter and her husband to use as an inn. Its date is probably close to 1840. The unusual spacing of the windows is due to the fact that the doorway opens into a good-sized, square lobby, behind which are the stairs in a separate hallway. The cross-division of the windows is due to storm sash. The inner sash is double-hung with the division into twenty-four panes usual in the earlier period.

19 *Former hotel, Normandale, Norfolk County*

Normandale was the site of one of the earliest iron smelters in Upper Canada, begun in 1816 and flourishing in the thirties and forties. This old inn probably dates from this prosperous period. There obviously were verandas in two storeys, masking the lack of symmetry between the two large doorways; the smaller door to the left will have led to the taproom or bar. The detail of the doorways with their one-panelled doors is of a kind found in this area in the later 1830s. The windows have been re-sashed at a much later period.

20 *St. Andrew's United Church, Grafton, Northumberland County*

St. Andrew's Church was built by Presbyterians in 1844, and still possesses its original communion silver. The style of the church seems to owe a good deal to Scottish examples of the post-Reformation period around 1600. In particular the design of the belfry with its overhang, battlements, and pinnacles can be paralleled from such examples, which are, of course, of stone. There has been some alteration in detail, particularly the glazing of the windows and the hood over the doorway, but the effect is much the same as when the church was built. A fine avenue of maples leads up to the door, and the surrounding churchyard is always well kept. Another Presbyterian church, on the Ottawa River near Grenville in Argenteuil County, P.Q., has some likeness to this one, but is built of stone without any spire.

21 *Stone farmhouse, on Highway 15, Pittsburgh Township, Frontenac County*

This house is very representative of a type to be found in almost every section of the province where quarried stone was easily obtainable. At first glance it might just as well be in Grenville or Lanark Counties as in Frontenac, though closer inspection shows difference of detail and material that would give a hint as to its location. Such houses are difficult to date by their appearance. The arched doorway looks a rather later version of a type in use from about 1830; the broad chimneys of the main block, however, indicate the presence of open fireplaces. The little 'ell' or back wing was obviously not built at the same time as the main block; its less careful masonry might suggest an earlier date, but it is more likely to be an addition. The windows have been resashed throughout, and a modern window inserted in the wing.

22 *Sharon burying ground, Sharon, York County*

A number of the Willsonites are buried in this cemetery, and it is possible that the doves on these stones have some reference to the 'Children of Peace'. The stones are more decorated than is usual with Quakers. Jacob Lundy, who became a follower of David Willson, was a member of a Quaker family who began a settlement near Pine Orchard in Whitchurch Township about 1800. The landscape in the background is characteristic of this part of Gwillimbury East, which is more gently rolling than much of the surrounding country.

BORN
Feb. 24. 1809.
DIED
June 3. 1878.

23 *Stone farmhouse, Williamsburgh Township, Dundas County*

This small farmhouse, on an old road running west from Williamsburg, was chosen partly because of its gaunt appearance and surroundings. Such a setting is, and probably always was to some extent, fairly common in Ontario. The house itself is also characteristic of its region. It has been resashed, but the size and shape of its windows suggest a fairly early date.

24 *The Richardson house, Whitchurch Township, York County*

This house is believed to have been built not long after 1840, and is in many respects typical of that period. The plan, however, is unusual in Ontario; it has some resemblance to a French-Canadian type. There is no hallway; the doorway in the end gives into the parlour, behind which to the right (east) is a good-sized living room with a large fireplace which once had a heavy chimney, now removed. Beside the chimney, a staircase winds down to the kitchen with its large fireplace, some bedrooms, and cellars. Other bedrooms are on the main floor and in the half storey. The house retains some of its original paintwork in the living room and parlour.

25 *The Thomson house, Queensborough, Hastings County*

Queensborough, in the sparsely inhabited township of Elzevir, is a small village at the end of a strip of farming country surrounded by metal-bearing rocks. This house was built about 1848 by the owner of the saw and grist mills which formed one of the main industries of the village. It is a very attractive example of what may be called 'Upper Canada Regency'. The trellis veranda echoes the balconies and narrow verandas found in some English cities, but other details are more local in character.

26 *Store and inn, Cashel, York County*

Cashel was an early centre in Markham Township with a Presbyterian church (later rebuilt further north), a post office, and some small industries. This brick inn is in the style usual around 1850. It may always have contained a store, but has certainly suffered some alterations and lost its veranda and the balcony which gave meaning to the upper doorway. The building beyond it to the right has the appearance of having been a carriage works, with the usual large doors in the upper storey. Cashel is no longer a post office, and can hardly be recognized as even a hamlet.

27 *Stone farmhouse, on Highway 2, Front of Leeds & Lansdowne Township, Leeds County*

Such stone houses as this one are to be found in limestone areas along the old main highway of the province. In this instance, certain details – the large twelve-paned lower windows, the square-headed doorway, and the small panes edging the side-lights, as well as the arched window in the peak – suggest a date close to, but probably after, 1850. It is possible that the veranda with its 'awning' curve, a fragment of which shows at the left, may have continued across the front. The local stone has a pleasant, warm colour, caused probably by iron in the strata.

28 *Christ Church Anglican, Vittoria, Norfolk County*

Archdeacon Bethune in his visitation in 1848 found this church in use, but not yet completely finished within. Its exterior, however, may be somewhat older. The style is unusual, being Italianate rather than Georgian. The covering of the church walls with flush boarding (once more strongly marked to resemble blocks of ashlar) and rusticated at the corners, was a not uncommon method at this time of giving monumentality to a wooden building. Although it disturbs purists, especially the followers of Ruskin, the effect in this case and in many others is decidedly pleasing.

29 *Grist mill, Brooklin, Ontario County*

This mill, still in use but no longer 'wrought by water', is an early example of a brick mill-building in Ontario. It is also interesting for the use of bricks to suggest mouldings in its entablature. The mill is even more impressive when viewed from below its old dam, but there is no date worked in the bricks of the other gable. Patterned brickwork of this type is far from common in Ontario, and it is curious to find it in conjunction with 'common bond'; the bricks themselves, however, appear to be handmade and are an excellent warm colour with pleasant variations of tone.

30 *The Major house, Pickering Township, Ontario County*

This fieldstone house east of Whitevale, originally called 'Major', was built by the Major family rather more than a century ago. The window over the door is a type found in several houses in Pickering and Markham townships, a Gothicized rendering of the Palladian window. The doorway, recessed in the thickness of the wall with panelled jambs and soffits, follows a design common in the 1860s, though the windows on either side of it are rather smaller than were usual at that period.

31 *The Wolverton house, Wolverton, Oxford County*

The founders of Wolverton were the second generation of a lumbering family, whose fine mansion stands in Paris, Ontario. They owned mills on the Nith River here and founded the village, building their big house in the 1850s. The house shows some features characteristic of its date, but others that are somewhat unusual. Casement windows in a house of Georgian type are not often found in this province outside the Ottawa Valley. The treatment of the deeply recessed porch is also uncommon, as is the pointed shape of the window in the gable. Combined with the rich colouring of the brick, these features make an unusually interesting composition.

1846
SHUR-GAIN
feed service
BROOKLIN
FLOUR MILLS
FEEDS

32 *United Church, Kirk Hill, Glengarry County*

Originally built by a Free Church group seceding from the older Church of Scotland parish of Lochiel in 1843, this church shows some mixture in style. A decided attempt has been made to gothicize the windows, but the tower and graceful spire are purely classic, particularly the urns at the corners. This type of spire supported by an eight-sided, open belfry was very commonly used in Upper Canada at a somewhat earlier date, but very few have survived unaltered.

33 *'Town Hall', Lang, Peterborough County*

For some reason this hall at Lang in Otonabee Township was known as the 'Town Hall', although Lang is only a medium-sized village and unincorporated. One story is that it was built in the hope that Lang might become a town; a more likely possibility is that Lang hoped to become the 'seat' of the township, for the building (destroyed some years ago) might well have been older than the township hall at Keene. The method of construction was unusual if the verticals were structural. It is more probable, however, that they represented pilasters, for there seems to have been a somewhat contracted entablature under the eaves, which was carried across the front gables as if it were a pediment. The whole arrangement was a countrified rendering of a 'temple design'.

34 *Pond and mill at Westwood, Peterborough County*

This grist mill on the River Ouse probably dates from the 1850s and was operated by water until a year or two ago. The dam is now used to control flow, which explains the low level of the pond. The concrete work is, of course, much more recent than the frame building and stone foundations. Those to the left once supported other mills using the same dam.

35 *Beaver Valley, Grey County*

This view from a point a little north of Eugenia Falls gives an excellent idea of the wide Beaver Valley, with its sides sloping up to bluffs or limestone cliffs, and covered with prosperous farms. In fact, from this point of view the proportion of woodland seems somewhat greater than is actually the case. The road in the distance leads towards Thornbury on the Georgian Bay.

36 *Bethesda United Church, Alnwick Township, Northumberland County*

This red brick church with buff brick buttresses at the corners has lost the wooden top of its little tower. Built in 1882, it is unusually simple in design for this late period. The farmhouse is a good deal older than the church. It is typical of the area and may date from the late 1850s; the pink stucco covering its dressed fieldstone will be still later. Beyond the hill with its little graveyard lies Rice Lake.

37 *View near Gore's Landing, Northumberland County*

This stretch of rolling country, extending north-west from the high ground on which a road runs from Gore's Landing westwards, is a fair sample of the scenery of this part of Northumberland County. The point of view is a little below the crest of the ridge which the road follows north of the 'Hamilton Plains', a stretch of hilly country once covered with open pine woods. The hills in the distance are beyond the westerly end of Rice Lake near Bewdley.

38 *Castle Hill Farm, Goulbourn Township, Carleton County*

The style of this house would suggest a date close to 1840, though possibly some allowance should be made for time lag. The upper doorway is a not uncommon feature in this part of the province, but is also found fairly frequently farther west. It may imply the former existence of a porch or veranda with a balcony above, but may also indicate an intention to add such a feature. The pool in the foreground is not simply flood water, but an artificial pond somewhat fuller than normal.

39 *View from Rattlesnake Point, Nelson Township, Halton County*

The valley enclosed by these two 'points' of the Niagara Escarpment shows the familiar pattern of much of Southern Ontario – a patchwork of fields varied by woods, 'shrubberies', and orchards; the fencerows marked in this case more by isolated trees than by continuous lines of bush or timber. It is this pattern which sometimes reminds people of the English countryside and which possesses some of the same settled charm. The metal roofs of the barns have been condemned by some, but they actually add an accent to the scene which would be missed if they were suddenly removed.

40 *Falls in the Beaver River, Eugenia, Grey County*

Eugenia Falls must have been magnificent before the water was diverted to run through penstocks and turn turbines to create electric power. As it is, the stream bed is often totally dry, but the gorge remains beautiful in spite of that. The Beaver River here flowed over the edge of limestone cliffs, and cut its way through the strata to a great depth. Such gorges, their crests and bluffs well wooded, are largely hidden from the roads and come as a surprise to the stranger who enters the parks that give access to them.

41 *Bridge over the Gananoque at Lyndhurst, Leeds County*

Fine stone bridges such as this one are something of a rarity in Ontario. It was built in 1856–57 under the direction of John Roddick. Lyndhurst was originally known as Furnace Falls, for the first iron smelter in Upper Canada was built here in 1801, and burned in 1811. It was replaced in 1833 by saw and grist mills, which were sold in the 1860s to Henry Green and John Roddick, who soon divided the property. The water privilege was divided by the little island seen in the photograph – Green having all the water that flowed under the two farther arches, and Roddick the water that passed under the near arch. The road which passes over the bridge was a highway built before 1800 from Kingston Mills to the Stevens settlement in Bastard Township, and later extended to Brockville. This road retained its importance even after the building of the first railways.

42 *St. Andrew's Presbyterian Church, Warsaw, Peterborough County*

It can be argued with a good deal of justice that this church built in 1856 represents a case of time lag in style. The windows most probably had small-paned sash corresponding to the interlacing glazing-bars in their heads, which are repeated in the doorway with its six-panelled door. Such features and the small tower with its pyramid roof recall certain churches built ten to fifteen years earlier. The plainness of the eaves, however, is a sign of later date, and gives the church a certain Calvinistic severity.

43 *Main street, Burritt's Rapids, Grenville County*

The three buildings in this photograph appear to be earlier than 1850, but only the one on the right has retained its original sash and a chimney large enough to contain fireplace flues. The doorway with side-lights and transom seems to be a later renewal, but the outer surround, with its over-slender pilasters supporting an elaborate entablature including a convex frieze, will be contemporary with the house. The low sills of the windows in the stone building indicate that it was built as a shop. The white clapboard house has suffered more alteration, but seems early. If the cantilevered balcony is the fragment of an old one extending across the front, and perhaps supported by posts from the sidewalk, this house may have been an inn.

ST ANDREW'S
PRESBYTERIAN
CHURCH
WARSAW

44 *Marshes, Presqu'ile Bay, Northumberland County*

Looking north from the Provincial Park towards Gosport in Brighton Township. The wooded ridge in the middle distance is a part of Presqu'ile Point, and the hills beyond are the morainic uplands extending towards the River Trent. Such bulrush beds as these provide plentiful feed for muskrats, and in season are (or were) an attraction for duck and other wildfowl. Large marshes of this kind are to be found in the Bay of Quinte and in other parts of Ontario.

45 *Roughcast house, Esquesing Township, Halton County*

The roughcast covering the walls of this house near Milton may be on stone rather than frame. The building is hard to date, for whatever its age it seems to hark back to a still older style. It may easily be no earlier than the late sixties. The five-bay front and the rather high hipped roof are reminiscent of early Georgian, but the vanished veranda seems to have had an awning curve. The four-pane sash in this case may be original. Whatever the date, the proportions are good.

46 *St. Anthony's Roman Catholic Church, South Easthope Township, Perth County*

The first Roman Catholic church in this area, now restored to its original condition and used for occasional services. This church represents a remarkable case of time lag. The detail of the doorway and of the three arched windows on either side would not be out of place on a building of forty years earlier than 1863. This might also be said of most of the other details – the simple cornice, the returned eaves, the treatment of the fieldstone masonry, and the sparing use of brickwork. Altogether this church seems particularly 'right' in every detail and proportion with the possible exception of the little cupola, which may have suffered some alteration. The setting is attractive and the churchyard well cared for.

1863

47 *Barnyard, Gore's Landing, Northumberland County*

This complex of barns was probably built at different dates. It is hard to say whether the large one in the background is older than the smaller barn at right angles to it, nor is it possible to guess the dates of any part of the complex, though it seems to be earlier than 1890, allowing for some improvement after 1900.

48 *Brick house, Foxboro, Hastings County*

It is a pity that some of the fretsaw-work has been removed from the end bays of the veranda and from the eaves of the roof, otherwise this house would well illustrate the type of 'Cottage Gothic' favoured in the late sixties and the seventies. The projecting porch in the centre gable seems to be an addition probably replacing a small balcony. A notable feature of the house is the presence of three entrance doors alternating with the windows of the ground floor. This unusual arrangement was found in a much older brick house standing in ruins by the Moira River, a little southeast of Foxboro, until a few years ago. In both cases, the reason for so many entrances is obscure.

49 *St. John's Lutheran Church, Wellesley Township, Waterloo County*

The same builder probably was responsible for this church and another Lutheran church, between Waterloo and St. Agatha, and the Roman Catholic church in PLATE 46. They all bear a strong family likeness, but this is the most recent of the three, dating from 1873. The late date is indicated in the carefully squared stonework, the simpler design of the windows, and the slightly unsure proportions of the entrance front. The spire, however, is the best of the three. The church stands high and commands splendid views over markedly rolling countryside.

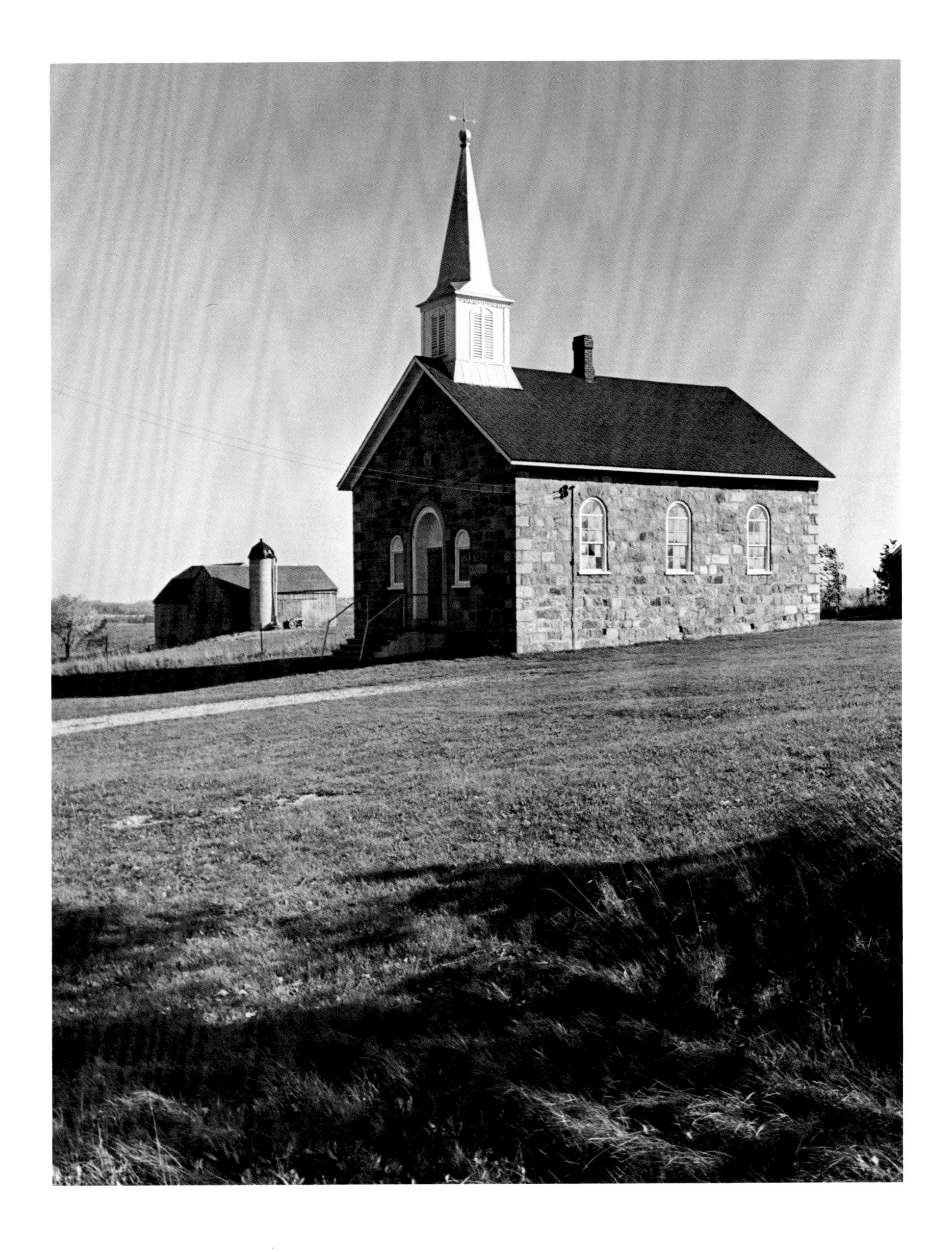

50 *Haldimand Township Hall, Grafton, Northumberland County*

This is a somewhat larger than usual example of a township hall, built probably in the 1860s. The proportions are on the whole good, especially those of the cupola, and the glazing, while using larger panes than in earlier examples, is still carefully in scale with the openings. The two windows to the right have recently been restored, replacing a store-front. It is possible that these arched openings once formed an arcade rather than windows.

51 *Street in Sheffield, Wentworth County*

Probably none of the three buildings in this picture is older than 1860, but they give a good impression of village grouping between 1830 and 1870. The house on the left with the two-storied veranda has all the marks of an hotel. Besides the double veranda, it has the second entrance door that probably gave access to the taproom; the more important doorway would have led to the hotel and family quarters. The upper balcony was intended for the use of ladies who might wish to shun the vicinity of the bar and the loiterers on the lower porch. The stone store building has what was known as an 'awning', once very common in villages, towns and cities. Until about 1880 most of the main street of Hamilton was lined with these permanent awnings.

52 *Concession road, Cramahe Township, Northumberland County*

Much of Northumberland County has a heavily rolling topography of morainic ridges and the isolated hills known as drumlins. The slopes are steep and the valleys are intricate and winding, though most of the area is good farmland. This results in views of great beauty and variety. The little church in the foreground is a late example and not particularly distinguished, but like many of the older buildings it seems to fit well into the landscape.

HALDIMAND TOWNSHIP
MUNICIPAL BUILDING

Drink
Coca-Cola
KIST

53 *Church and schoolhouse, South Bay, Prince Edward County*

This little schoolhouse originally stood beside an earlier Methodist church finished about 1859–60. Ten years later, in 1870, the older church was burnt and the present church begun in 1871. The round arches and wheel-window used here are not a return to an earlier classical manner, but reflect the current liking for forms of Romanesque, with a suggestion in this case of Italian origin.

54 *The MacGillivray house, Kirk Hill, Glengarry County*

It is at first glance difficult to say whether this house, almost opposite the United Church (PLATE 32), dates from the 1860s or is an earlier house embellished at that period. The lack of symmetry, the long, low line, and the rather small windows point to an earlier date, but the detail of the doorway and of the triple windows in the peaks seems more likely to belong after 1865. As the peaks appear to be framed and not of stone, they at least may be embellishments. These arched windows might be compared with the one in the house in PLATE 30, with which they may be nearly contemporary. The sash of the lower windows is, of course, late. Asymmetrical houses of this kind, with four openings instead of three or five, are more common to the east than to the west of the Trent.

55 *Fruit barn, Echo Hall, Grimsby, Lincoln County*

A specialized variety of barn, found in the Niagara Peninsula, used for storing and packing fruit. The style is that of the 1870s, a form of cottage Gothic distinguished from the style of the 1850s not only by greater vertical emphasis, but by the fact that the barge-boards and eaves ornament are fretsawed in loops and scrolls rather than built up in Gothic cusps and pendants. The use of vertical siding (here board-and-batten) is common to both periods.

56 *Flour mill, Baltimore, Northumberland County*

A good specimen of the large framed flour mill once numerous in Ontario. There are indications that this mill may have been built in two sections, in which case the older one to the right may predate 1850. There was a mill here much earlier than that, but it was probably smaller though likely to have been framed. In spite of resashing the whole building has retained a good deal of its early look. The interiors of such mills are very impressive, especially when they retain some of their old machinery.

57 *Wagon shop, Walsingham Township, Norfolk County*

The main part of this fine example of board-and-batten construction, on the shore road just west of Big Creek in Walsingham Township, seems to have been a wagon or carriage factory, but the lean-to extension to the left, which makes the outline so picturesque, may possibly have been a smithy. The smith's and wheelwright's trades were often combined and frequently developed into the manufacture of wagons, sleighs, and even carriages. Carriage shops almost always have a second pair of double doors in an upper storey, allowing the vehicles to be hoisted to a loft for storage or painting. It is rare, however, to find such a shop with so satisfying a 'saltbox' roof.

58 *Paris Plains Church, South Dumfries Township, Brant County*

The West Dumfries Chapel or Paris Plains Church was built in 1845 by the Methodists. It is one of three churches in Ontario built of cobblestones. This method of building with small stones resembles the flint building in England, where cobbles are also used occasionally in this manner. There are two groups of cobblestone buildings in this province – one in and near Paris, and another near Belleville. The Paris group more often shows this elaborate herringbone design between marked ridges, similar to examples in northern New York State, and is, indeed, said to have been introduced by a builder from that area named Levi Boughton. The doors in this example are much later than the church.

Swift's FEEDS
CUSTOM
GRINDING MIXING SAWING
GRASS SEEDS · SEED CORN
FENCING · POULTRY EQUIPMENT
GRAINS FOR SALE HERE

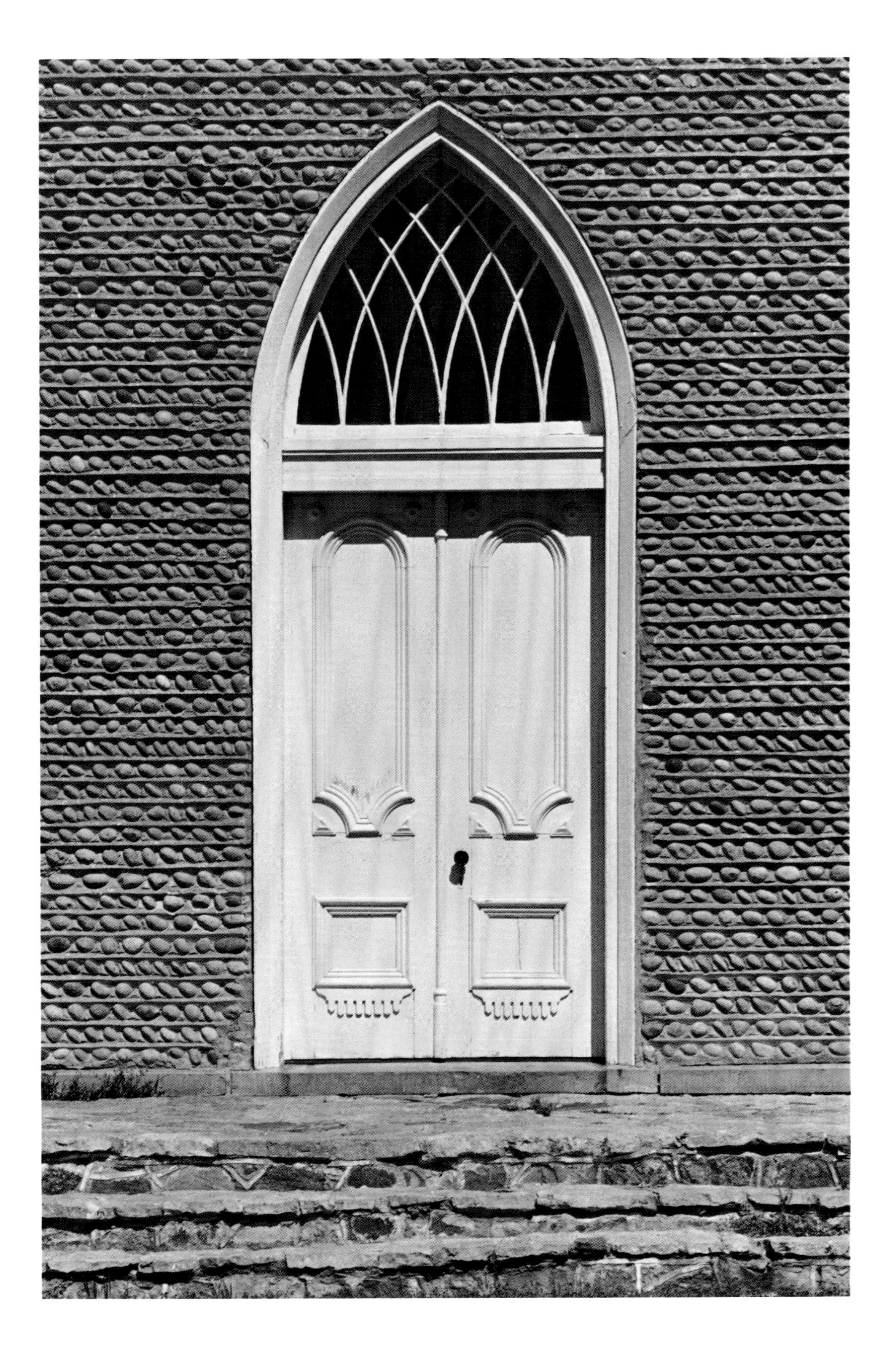

59 *Sophiasburgh Township Hall, Demorestville, Prince Edward County*

The habit of referring to townships as 'towns' was brought by the first settlers from New England and continued in this area to a late date. This hall bears the marks of the late sixties or early seventies. The segmental arches, fretwork decoration, and enlarged door transom belong to that period. Demorestville was once a place of considerable importance, and until recently contained a number of fine but decayed houses, most of which have been repaired without much regard to their original character.

60 *The Peter Duncan house, North Norwich Township, Oxford County*

The area near and west of the Grand River contains a number of houses built in a late version of the Greek Revival style, though not usually showing as much departure from the normal as this one. In its present state with the front painted in one tone of red, the house is impressive and pleasing. An old photograph shows it as it was when built in 1857 with pilasters and voussoirs of staring white brick. This sharp contrast in colour over-emphasized the verticals and upset the proportions, giving the building a much more Victorian look. The Greek Doric porch with its slightly attenuated pillars is characteristic of this area, and the Gothic tracery in the round-arched window is also not uncommon.

61 *United Church, Hazzard's Corners, Hastings County*

Hazzard's Corners in Madoc Township is located on one of the strips of fairly good farmland that run into the rocky Laurentian Shield in this and the adjoining townships. The existence of this agricultural strip would hardly be suspected by travellers along Highway 7 a few miles to the south of it. The United Church was built by Methodists in 1857, and widened later without harming its attractive outline. As a result of the enlargement, the interior has two rows of posts forming aisles, and an unusual ceiling. The builder has managed with very simple means to produce a building of great charm slightly suggesting the Gothic style, but with a doorway that is purely Neo-classic. The drive-shed was once a regular adjunct to country churches, and in this case groups very well with the church and well-kept graveyard.

TOWN HALL

62 *Staff cottages, Greenfield, near Ayr, Waterloo County*

Company housing on this scale is not particularly common in Ontario before 1870. These cottages probably date from the 1860s, for they lack a few features usual in the forties and fifties, and appear to have been heated by stoves. They make an attractive row along the single street of this little mill village, with the mill-owner's mansion on the opposite side of the road.

63 *Flour mill, Elora, Wellington County*

This large stone building, a hundred feet high, on the brink of the falls on the Grand River, was built in 1866 to replace a frame flour mill of considerable size which had been destroyed by fire. In both cases the buildings contained a saw-mill. A partial collapse of the gable necessitated the conspicuous patching with timber. Unlike many surviving mills, this one is still operated by water, though it is now used for chopping feed rather than grinding.

64 *Lake Ontario from the Lakeshore Road, Clarke Township, Durham County*

Shore erosion along this stretch of Lake Ontario has increased the height of the clay cliffs and gullying has taken place at many points, sometimes producing even larger ravines than this one. These gullies so distressing to the conservationist can be very pleasing to the casual traveller, especially when, as on this occasion, the lake is a rich and deep blue contrasting with the whiteness of the birch trees and the soft grey of the clay point. Much of the first Grand Trunk Railway between Oshawa and Cobourg was laid out so close to the water's edge that the whole line had to be moved inland about forty years after it was finished in 1856. Near this point the Lakeshore Road has recently been moved back further than the railway. Erosion is still continuing here to some extent.

65 *'Stone Church', Sidney Township, Hastings County*

Most of the cobblestone buildings in the vicinity of this church may perhaps be attributed to the same builder. This may have been a stonemason named Wickett who is known to have done the masonry of the church. The technique differs considerably from the better-known group of cobblestone work in and near Paris, Ontario, and some people may feel that the slighter emphasis on the pointing of the joints between courses of cobbles produces a more satisfactory surface. It is notable that the arches are constructed in true mason-fashion with stone voussoirs, whereas in at least some of the Paris examples they are simply shaped holes in the wall (see PLATE 58). Now United, the 'Stone Church' was built by Wesleyan Methodists in 1853–55. It is no longer in use and is threatened with destruction.

66 *Farmhouse, on Highway 8, Goderich Township, Huron County*

The thickness of the walls of this stuccoed house suggests masonry, probably of brick. Located on the Huron Road, it may well be later in date than it appears, probably well into the 1850s at least. In another area the details could suggest an earlier date. The eared window architraves and pilastered doorway hint at the Greek Revival, though the pilasters are decidedly attenuated and their entablature simplified. The house has retained its original glazing throughout, partly disguised in front by double windows.

67 *Schoolhouse, Meadowvale, Peel County*

An attractive example of the later type of schoolhouse, probably built to conform to the specifications published by Egerton Ryerson in his magazine. The handling of the board-and-batten is slightly more sophisticated than is often the case, with the battens dying into small segmental arches under the eaves. The over-narrow windows are characteristic of the time. The plaque in the gable (now removed) gives the date as 1871. The building is now used as a community hall.

SCHOOL SECTION
No 13
A.D. 1871.

68 *United Church, North Gower, Carleton County*

Built in 1870, this church hardly shows a detail, including the false clock-faces, that might not have been produced twenty years earlier. The curious practice of painting clocks on churches and halls was not uncommon in Ontario, and where there is more than one face it is not unusual for each to show a different hour. Why the painter selected the hours shown here is anybody's guess. The spire and belfry, although the opening of the latter are closed with louvres, hark back to the very early type. There is scarcely a trace of the elaborate 'carpenter's' Gothic which was normal at this period in church-building.

69 *Frame house, Lochiel Township, Glengarry County*

At first glance this is a mid-Victorian building of a type rather common in the extreme eastern part of Ontario and resembling certain houses in Quebec. The distinguishing features are the flat, or nearly flat, roof, the projecting bracketed cornice, the veranda supported on turned posts, and the triple window with all three lights arched. However, a closer inspection reveals under the veranda twelve-paned windows with pilastered architraves in a much earlier manner, and it is possible that a storey-and-a-half house has been converted to two storeys at some time just before or just after 1870.

70 *Trinity the Marsh Anglican Church, Cavan Township, Durham County*

This little church stands isolated in the extreme western edge of Cavan Township and serves a part of Manvers Township as well as a part of Cavan. The building is in a style favoured by the Anglicans in the seventies and eighties. It is probably the one marked on a township plan of 1878. The 'marsh' is now largely drained, but farther south on the townline between Cavan and Manvers some fragments of it are blue in season with wild iris.

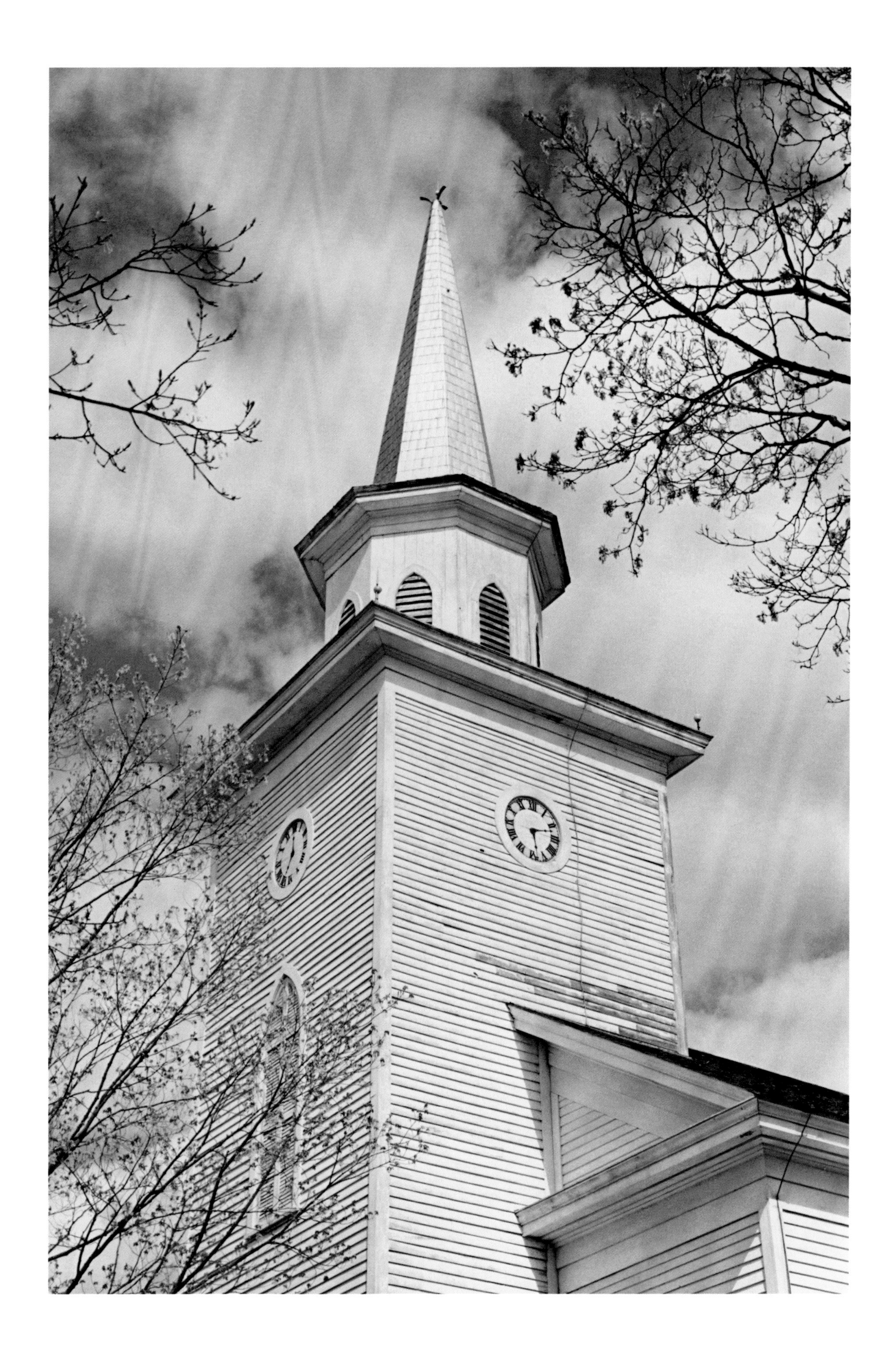

71 *Frame farmhouse, Markham Road (Highway 48) Borough of Scarborough, Metropolitan Toronto*

Although part of Metropolitan Toronto, 'Brown's Corners' is still semi-rural, and when this photograph was taken ten years ago was decidedly so. The house is in the full style of about 1880 – a style developed from the cottage Gothic of the late 1840s, but retaining in its fretted and spindled gable very little that can be called Gothic. The upper window, however, does at least have a pointed arch. The segmentally curved tops of the lower windows are features carried over from the 1860s. The narrow vertical siding covering the walls began to be used very early by the settlers in Markham, and is also found in this part of Scarborough.

72 *Barns, North Dumfries Township, Waterloo County*

Such wide-spreading barns with lean-to 'aisles' on either side are frequently found in Waterloo County. As is usual, the south aisle is an overhang open below; it is cut short by the ell on the west. The barn may be of several dates, possibly enclosing a frame of some age. The long, low, stone building looks as though it might have begun life as a piggery, at least in part.

73 *Loyal Orange Lodge, Campbellville, Halton County*

Lodges of the Loyal Orange Order were once very numerous in Ontario, but are becoming less so. They can usually be recognized by the fact that their windows are either closed with solid shutters, or as here with whitewashed glass. This example with its arched openings and the interlacing glazing-bars of its sashes is more sophisticated in design than many, for lodges often look like very plain school-houses.

LOL
NO 1184

74 *Store, Lakefield, Peterborough County*

Stores of this kind are occasionally found in small rural villages, or even isolated at cross-roads, but this example is in a larger place. It is an interesting 1880 or 1890 version of a type more common in the 1860s. The mansard roof, dormers, and segmental-headed windows belong to the post-Civil-War style, but the details have been transformed in a manner that may well have been suggested by *The Woodworker*, a magazine published in Grand Rapids, apparently to popularize the various kinds of millwork that might be used in building.

75 *View north from Highway 7 near Greenwood, Ontario County*

This stretch of country with its ring of low hills, often appearing heightened by clear weather until they seem mountains, is reasonably representative of the morainic country which extends along the north shore of Lake Ontario at varying distances inland. At any season it has great beauty of its own kind, a beauty which has not always been fully appreciated.

76 *Barns, Puslinch Township, Wellington County*

This barn complex, well maintained and obviously efficient, may yet include parts that have seen a century of use. The farm has been occupied for a hundred years or more by the same family. The gambrel roof of the ell and other features obviously represent more recent improvements; the frames may be much older. Its whole air suggests capable farming.

GROCERIES
SPENCE & SONS
CHINAWARE
VEGETABLES
Drink Coca-Cola
Drink Coca-Cola
GROCERIES
SALADA

77 *Rosemont School, on Highway 89, Mono Township, Dufferin County*

Two-roomed schoolhouses are not often found in the countryside, and few have remained for seventy and eighty years with so little alteration. This may perhaps be attributed to the soundness of the building. The builder has followed contemporary fashion to some extent without going to extreme. The school shows that tendency to increased height which is noticeable in all Ontario buildings in the last half of the nineteenth century and which rarely helps the proportions; it is due as a rule to increased ceiling heights without an increase in the size of rooms. This may possibly be the result of heating by stoves or furnaces, which made the rooms seem stuffy to those used to open fires.

78 *St. Columba's Presbyterian Church, Kirk Hill, Glengarry County*

The body of this church was built in 1863–65 to replace one begun in 1822 to serve a congregation in connection with the Kirk of Scotland organized in 1819. The name St. Columba's was adopted for Lochiel Parish in 1862. The spire was added in 1889. The church retains the plainness of earlier buildings very suitable to the Presbyterian character, but the tower and spire to some extent represent the more scholarly Gothic which had already become usual when this church was begun. In spite of its austerity the building has a dignity worthy of its position on the hilltop overlooking a wide stretch of country.

79 *Farm, on Highway 6, Normanby Township, Grey County*

An attractive example of an Ontario farmstead; the buildings are close to each other in age, which in the case of the house seems to be about ninety years or more. The location chosen for the buildings is somewhat unusual, being some distance from the road and on the crest of a ridge. Somewhat earlier, the farm would have been more likely to have sheltered below the slope, and many farmers might have preferred a shorter lane.

R.D.MORTON

80 *Farm, Clarke Township, Durham County*

Another farmstead of about the same age as the last, but separated from it by more than a hundred miles. For more than twenty years this farm has been well maintained and apparently prosperous. Although the ground appears level, the farm is on the top of a high drumlin. Drumlins are composed of a good till soil which may, however, be full of glacial boulders.

81 *Old hotel, Goodwood, Ontario County*

This inn has a great air of age, but we have a travelling missionary's word for it that there were no houses on this early road from Uxbridge to Stouffville in 1831. The inn may date from about 1840; Michael Chapman was innkeeper and postmaster at Goodwood in 1857. However, Goodwood is essentially a 'railway village', its growth stimulated by the Toronto and Nipissing Railway – a narrow-gauge line opened about 1870.

82 *View looking west, Sidney Township, Hastings County*

This is a landscape of south-central Ontario at its most characteristic. Rolling country ending in higher ridges and covered with a patchwork of fields and fencerow timber dotted with barns. The number of rail fences still surviving is noticeable, particularly to the left of the road in the middle distance. In the far distance are some high hills beyond the Trent in Northumberland County.

83 *Road bridge over old Midland Railway line (now* CNR*), Rawdon Township, Hastings County*

This bridge is probably of no great age, having been renewed many times since the railway was built, but it is interesting because it perpetuates a method of building bridges that was very common in the early days of Upper Canada. By this method a series of timber-framed 'bents' was erected at proper intervals, and long stringers laid across from one bent to another to carry the roadway. The bents were braced diagonally, as these ones are, and braces also ran from bent to stringer giving an effect of arches. The type of long braces used here would, of course, only be possible at the banks and not in the stream itself.

84 *Cheese factory, Camden Township, Lennox & Addington County*

The first cheese factories were opened in 1866 and in the next years multiplied with extreme rapidity. In the last decades their number has dwindled almost equally quickly. This one, which probably dates from rather late in the last century, was evidently running quite recently, but is now closed and for sale. With its loading platform, overhanging canopy, and ventilators, it is reasonably representative of the type.

85 *Farmhouse, Dereham Township, Oxford County*

The details of this house suggest a date about 1880, although its shape and plan could be earlier. It is a very full-blown example of late Victorianism, from its cast 'stone' keystones moulded with Scotch thistles to the elaborate patterning of its slate roof in three colours. Compare the heavy brackets under the eaves here with others on some earlier houses illustrated. Light brick is often used after 1850 to set off detail against red brick walls; it is here handled with considerable skill. The house has lost some kind of porch which was topped with a balcony, but otherwise seems little changed from the time of its building.

FOR SALE

86 *Store building, Bethany, Durham County*

This little false-fronted building would attract notice by its small size even without its elaborate porch. The latter, however, is a full version of the type common in the 1880s and 90s, involving a good deal of turned work in posts, spindles, etc. Such detail was used indoors, particularly in arches between rooms, and in the head of ordinary doorways. The rods piercing balls which make up the quadrant fans are very common in this interior work, but all varieties of spindles occur. The square false front, of course, is used to mask the gable of a pitched roof and give greater importance to a shop front by giving it greater height.

87 *Barn group, Hope Township, Durham County*

This great barn falls into at least two sections built, it would seem, about thirty years apart. The barn to the right has cut in its gable two dates – the upper one reading from right to left appears to be 1858, while below it, in smaller figures reading from left to right, is cut 1885. Apparently the sheeting boards were taken off, turned over, re-used and a new date cut out. Whether we should deduce from this that the large wing extending westwards (left) dates from 1885 is not entirely clear. Its deep overhang supported on extremely massive cedar posts would at that date be an old-fashioned feature. The purpose of the little gable in this wing is obscure; it is not, as is usually the case, intended to give greater height to doors opening on the threshing floor. Whatever the dates, the whole complex is unusual and interesting.

88 *Brick house, Blackstock, Durham County*

This house, in a village which at one time promised to be of some size, was built probably after 1875 by a Doctor Montgomery. Until 1966 it continued to be occupied by medical men, and the word 'surgery' is still written in large letters over the door leading from the veranda to the room with a bay window. The house in its general plan and outline follows the 'Tuscan villa' type of some twenty years earlier, but the details are those of the current style. It has been little changed externally and has even retained the fretsaw drops between the brackets of the veranda; but these have been painted green and do not show in the photograph. Although this is a village house, its grounds back on the open country as can be seen in the picture.

BETHANY
POST
OFFICE

89 *School at Lonsdale, Hastings County*

This schoolhouse of 1873 shows the influence of contemporary building fashions in some of its details, but in general resembles the type in use since the sixties. It is still in use but will probably not be so much longer, for the consolidation of schools has resulted in most of the old one-roomed schoolhouses being converted into dwellings or destroyed. Lonsdale is a mill village that either never grew up to its surveyed town-plot, or has been in greater part torn down. Judging by the masses of lilac bushes along the half-deserted streets, the latter is the more probable explanation. When in bloom, these lilacs are a sight worth seeing.

90 *Farmhouse, Nassagaweya Township, Halton County*

The appearance of this house places it at once in the third quarter of the nineteenth century. The careful dressing of the fieldstone, the height of the walls to the eaves, the fretwork barge-boards, and steep-pitched roofs, all produce a sober Victorianism that has not yet become fantastic. The glazed porch, needed because this house faces north, is decidedly well-designed, and, in spite of a slight tendency to look too tall, the house still satisfies the eye. In this view, it looks perhaps a little forlorn and lost in the wintry landscape, as Ontario farmhouses sometimes do, especially those built after 1870.

List of Photographs

77 Rosemont School, on Highway 89, Mono Township, Dufferin County (1959)
78 St. Columba's Presbyterian Church, Kirk Hill, Glengarry County (1965)
79 Farm, on Highway 6, Normanby Township, Grey County (1965)
80 Farm, Clarke Township, Durham County (1967)
81 Old hotel, Goodwood, Ontario County (1966)
82 View looking west, Sidney Township, Hastings County (1967)
83 Road bridge over old Midland Railway Line (now CNR), Rawdon Township, Hastings County (1967)
84 Cheese factory, Camden Township, Lennox & Addington County (1967)
85 Farmhouse, Dereham Township, Oxford County (1967)
86 Store building, Bethany, Durham County (1968)
87 Barn group, Hope Township, Durham County (1967)
88 Brick house, Blackstock, Durham County (1968)
89 School at Lonsdale, Hastings County (1967)
90 Farmhouse, Nassagaweya Township, Halton County (1967)

Index

I

J K

L

M

N

P

This book
was designed by
ALLAN FLEMING
with the assistance of
LAURIE LEWIS
The photographic plates
were prepared by
HERZIG SOMERVILLE LTD
and the book
was printed by
HALLIDAY LITHOGRAPH
CORPORATION
for
University of
Toronto
Press